Follow My Lead

WHAT TRAINING MY DOGS TAUGHT ME ABOUT LIFE, LOVE, AND HAPPINESS

Carol Quinn

SEAL PRESS

Follow My Lead

What Training My Dogs Taught Me About Life, Love, and Happiness

Copyright © 2011 by Carol Quinn

Published by
Seal Press
A Member of the Perseus Books Group
1700 Fourth Street
Berkeley, California

Library of Congress Cataloging-in-Publication Data

Quinn, Carol.
  Follow my lead : what training my dogs taught me about life, love, and happiness / Carol Quinn.
      p. cm.
  Includes bibliographical references and index.
  ISBN-13: 978-1-58005-370-9 (pbk.)
  ISBN-10: 1-58005-370-X
  1. Dogs—Training—Anecdotes. 2. Dogs—Behavior—Anecdotes. 3. Human-animal relationships—Anecdotes. 4. Human-animal communication—Anecdotes. I. Title.
  SF426.2.Q85 2011
  636.7'0835—dc22
                                      2011006587

9 8 7 6 5 4 3 2 1

Cover and interior design by Domini Dragoone
Interior photographs © Rich Marchewka
Printed in the United States of America
Distributed by Publishers Group West

The author has changed some names and personal details to protect the privacy of those mentioned in the book.

To Andrea

"One can't say how life is, how chance or fate

deals with people, except by telling the tale."

—HANNA ARENDT
May 31, 1971

On Dogs

"Don't accept your dog's admiration as conclusive evidence that you
are wonderful."
—ANN LANDERS

"Any woman who does not thoroughly enjoy tramping across the
country on a clear frosty morning with a good gun and a pair of dogs
does not know how to enjoy life."
—ANNIE OAKLEY

"Dogs feel very strongly that they should always go with you in the
car, in case the need should arise for them to bark violently at nothing
right in your ear."
—DAVE BARRY

"A dog doesn't care if you're rich or poor, big or small, young or old.
He doesn't care if you're not smart, not popular, not a good joke-teller,
not the best athlete, nor the best-looking person. To your dog, you are
the greatest, the smartest, the nicest human being who was ever born.
You are his friend and protector."
—LOUIS SABIN

"You ask of my companions. Hills, sir, and the sundown, and a dog as large as myself that my father bought me. They are better than human beings, because they know but do not tell."
—EMILY DICKINSON

"The great pleasure of a dog is that you may make a fool of yourself with him and not only will he not scold you, but he will make a fool of himself too."
—SAMUEL BUTLER

"Dogs don't know about beginnings, and they don't speculate on matters that occurred before their time. Dogs also don't know— or at least don't accept—the concept of death. With no concept of beginnings or endings dogs probably don't know that for people having a dog as a life companion provides a streak of light between two eternities of darkness."
—STANLEY COREN

Contents

Introduction

Throughout my life, there has been one constant: dogs. I've had good dogs, neurotic dogs, silly dogs, dumb dogs, and great dogs—but they all shared one thing in common: They each taught me something. My two Rhodesian ridgebacks, Nairobi and Sheila, were my finest teachers. Perhaps these two dogs had such a profound effect on me because of timing. I had raised two sons alone; one was already in college, and my youngest had that faraway—*Yay! College! Freedom!*—look in his eye.

I believe I had the same look in my eye—at least the freedom part—but I am a nurturer at heart. When suddenly there wasn't a child relying on me for guidance, coaching, love, and affection, it was unsettling.

Enter the ridgebacks.

Though these dogs needed my love, care, and instruction, for the first time in my life I was fully able to listen to what they had to share with me.

I finally had the time to experience the extraordinary nature of dogs—and the good judgment to incorporate their practical wisdom into my life.

More specifically, my dogs were *ridgebacks*. Rhodesian ridgebacks are the breed of dog closest to my understanding of people; they're independent and stubborn. Bred in South Africa to track lions and to guard family farms and ranches, they are both aggressive protection animals and lazy hounds that like to nap in the sun. Ridgebacks are a bit of a conundrum; dutiful and reliable, they can also be quite silly and impulsive. One thing they are not is compliant. Their personalities remind me of intractable middle managers or headstrong artists. Ask them to sit and they will stare at you in return. It won't be an aggressive look. It's more—thoughtful.

Sit? Really? Are you sure that's what you want?

In that moment before the ridgeback sits—or doesn't—you are looking into the eyes of an animal that needs to decide for itself whether he or she wants to sit for you.

I can relate to that look. I have a lot in common with my ridgebacks. How interesting, then, that our obstinate, autonomous "pack" ended up in dog agility—the one sport where stubbornness isn't an asset and independence will get you nowhere.

When I told a friend one day that I couldn't meet for coffee because I had an agility class, there was a long pause before he finally asked, "Why? Are you stiff?"

Having ridden horses throughout my life, agility seemed exactly like a hunter jumper course, the difference being that you run beside the dog instead of sitting on the horse. Since control over the dog is limited to voice and hand signals (no leashes), the burden is on the relationship between dog and handler. At its best, when dog and handler are working in concert, the experience of teamwork can be extraordinary. It can be a total high when it goes well. When it goes badly, it's awful—like dancing with a partner who keeps stepping on your toes.

Here's a description of agility from the United States Dog Agility Association:

> *Dog agility is a competitive sport that tests a person's skills in training and handling of dogs over a timed obstacle course. Competitors race against the clock as they direct their dogs to jump hurdles, scale ramps, burst through tunnels, traverse a see-saw and weave through a line of poles in an obstacle course configuration designed to challenge a handler's competitive and training skills. With scoring based on faults similar to equestrian show jumping, dog agility has become an exciting spectator event.*

Okay, that's the technical description. But honestly, this can be a hilarious sport when things go awry on the course. There is nothing funnier than watching red-faced women and men chase their dogs, crash into obstacles, and stumble into inelegant falls. Sometimes the dog goes one way, the handler another, and they stare at one another across the field—both looking surprised and confused. *How did you get over there?*

The dogs, for their part, give their owners perplexed looks if they're sent in the wrong direction, and look equally perplexed—even hurt—if handlers act frustrated or lose their tempers. "Isn't this supposed to be fun?" the dogs seem to be asking.

Yes. It's supposed to be fun. But it only gets fun when you get good at it or at least get used to accepting failure and surrendering to the joy that can be found in the sheer effort of trying. To excel at agility you need to be kind, patient, clear-headed, and fairly self-deprecating. If anything goes wrong, which it usually does, it's your responsibility. The dog is just following directions.

I ended up in dog agility partly because I wanted to have some fun with my young, spirited dog Nairobi. Though I wasn't conscious of it at the time, it was also an escape from a complex romantic relationship that was dominating my life. On the surface, everything was fine; my advertising agency was flourishing, I had begun work on a novel, and I was in a committed relationship with my boyfriend, Henry. But something was off. My big love was turning out to be smaller than I'd hoped for. I didn't see it—I felt it. Too many arguments, breakups, and strained silences had accumulated between us. I was frustrated, restless, but I ignored my feelings. When I did focus on what was happening between Henry and me, I simply vowed to try harder. I forged on. I overrode my instincts.

Then I met my teacher, Irina, and things unfolded quite differently than I'd planned.

Irina: renowned agility handler and teacher, Eastern European, funny, experienced, well-traveled, a bit of a philosopher, compassionate, loving in a tough-love way, completely in tune with dogs—slightly wary of humans. Irina was always very nice to my dogs. "Nice" isn't the word I'd choose to describe her interactions with me, but I matured under her constant challenges to my misconceptions about animals, myself, and the people in my life. She taught me more than dog-handling skills, more than just how to understand the animals under my care and be a more responsible pet owner—she helped me form a blueprint for the right way to live.

For five years, I studied and practiced the sport of dog agility. I began with Nairobi when he was a year-and-a-half, and when his five-month-old cousin, Sheila, joined our family, she began training with us when she was mature enough. I don't enjoy competition so we never competed in the sport. We just studied together. We're still studying. Both dogs have thrived. And so have I, though as I occasionally fall hard in the dirt or chase after one or the other of the dogs that has taken off after a squirrel, I'd say I'm still learning.

I'm making a "good effort," Irina would say.

Classes began around Nairobi and Sheila—two wonderfully different and complex dogs—but as time went on, it occurred to me that I was the one being trained.

Bit by bit, the dogs trained me.

Class after class, Irina trained me.

The parallels between what I was teaching the dogs and what I was learning about myself became too clear to ignore. As I tried to understand how dogs think or how they're motivated, I began to admire the utilitarian simplicity of a dog's life. Clearly, they had a lot to teach me about living simply, with deep enjoyment, and acceptance. And in my conversations with Irina, I began a journey of self-discovery and self-mastery that would impact every area of my life.

Agility became a metaphor for life.

Obstacles became challenges to overcome.

Handling my dogs became a test for my strength, commitment, bravery, and creativity as a person.

Dog behavior became a guide for following my instincts and using my common sense.

Training my dogs became a way to train myself to become a confident, assured leader, and to assume the position of the alpha dog in my own life—to follow my own lead.

Know Your Dog

chapter one

To excel in dog agility, you have to know your dog—
his personality, limitations, and motivation.

In reality, it's fairly easy to know a dog.
A dog already knows who he is.

People are a bit more complicated.
We often disguise our nature—even to ourselves.

At the beginning of a new chapter in life, you don't have enough information to truly assess how a potential experience might affect your day-to-day life or impact your future. But that has never stopped me from trying. Whether it was having children, falling in love with a complex, difficult man, or bringing a dog into my life, I began the process with tremendous enthusiasm—and very big dreams.

When my boys were born, my imagination ran wild. *This child is uniquely gifted! He'll play the violin, excel in sports, and go to Stanford!* But every child is a complete unknown, a mystery; you can hardly imagine who that child is or will become—and how that child will change you.

As my sons grew, and I began to know and understand them, my fantasies about who they would become simply faded into memory. I deferred to their natures; I accepted that they were completely—and authentically—themselves.

They did prove to be uniquely gifted—just not on the violin.

When I first began dating Henry, I was swept away with the sheer romance of "us." Our relationship was madly passionate, and I believed our love was destined for greatness. *We'll both write best-selling novels, move to Europe, and host fascinating dinner parties! We'll speak fluent French and Italian!* As our relationship developed, though, there were signs that my vision of our potential was highly exaggerated. Whatever wonderful qualities we had as individuals, as a couple, we were nowhere near wonderful.

I showed good sense when it came to accepting my sons true selves, but with Henry, I stubbornly held fast to my original idea of who I thought he was—or wanted him to be.

But you can't ever fathom what a relationship will come to mean to you. You can't see the end at the beginning.

You can only have the experience.

I HAD BIG DREAMS FOR every dog I've owned, too. *We'll take long hikes together, embark on amazing adventures! I'll train these dogs perfectly!*

This was especially true of my Rhodesian ridgebacks, Nairobi and Sheila.

But every cute puppy is also a complete unknown. And you can hardly imagine what that dog will become, or how that dog will change you.

The only thing you can be sure of is that it will be an adventure.

A DOG SHOW AND SHOWING-UP ARE TWO VERY DIFFERENT THINGS

Before I started dog agility, I made a short, awkward detour into the dog show world. All the littermates of my young dog, Nairobi—who was just over a year old—were beginning to rack up their American Kennel Club championship points, and my breeder put the pressure on to start showing Nairobi.

Competition makes me anxious, but having my dog judged was even harder to contemplate.

And frankly, I had good reason to be insecure about submitting Nairobi to the scrutiny of the AKC judges.

My dog had a very big flaw.

In most respects, Nairobi is a perfectly formed, beautiful example of a Rhodesian ridgeback. He has a deep red coat, one white paw, and a white-and-black spotted chest, which is permissible in the AKC definition of the breed. He's a compact, muscular male, not huge, but breed standard with a perfect ridge running down his back. He happens to have a goofy personality, but that shouldn't disqualify him from anything. What set him apart were his ears. When he was about six months old, his ears started to "sprout" (a kind description)—outward. Most ridgebacks have long, smooth ears that lay flat to the head, but occasionally a puppy will be born with unruly ears—like Nairobi's. I didn't realize I was supposed to tape his ears under his snout so that they would grow properly. By the time my breeder told me about the taping, Nairobi's ears had already done a pretty good job of growing outward, so that when he cocked his head, the sight resembled the cornette that Sally Fields wore as the title character on the television show *The Flying Nun*. I tried taping, but it was too late, and honestly, the whole process reminded me of Chinese foot binding. I wasn't all that into it. As a result, Nairobi's ears took on a life of their own. My breeder advised me to have him wear a special hat that would help correct the problem, but one look at his miserable face, and I decided that Nairobi's ears would just have to be his unique attribute. Still, every time I saw his ears take flight, my heart sank. It was like the first time one of my sons wasn't liked or accepted, or wasn't deemed as successful as his peers. From preschool to high school, I'd fought the competitive mother syndrome. I tried to resist both the impulse to brag when my kids accomplished something and the feeling of shame when my kids exhibited any deficits. To a certain degree I succeeded with my children, but here I was with my dog, caught up in the same kind of competitive pressure. It's a character-defining moment when you accept that your child isn't perfect, yet you still have the will to encourage the best in them.

And it's a character-defining moment when you realize that your dog has ears that make him look like the Flying Nun.

So, ears and all, I bucked-up and enrolled Nairobi in a handler class to prepare for our first show. The class was held in a parking lot deep in the San Fernando Valley. It was close to sunset when we arrived, and when Nairobi and I got out of the car, we were faced with ten gorgeous Rhodesian ridgebacks and their owners. Nairobi lifted his head up, sniffed the air, and then bounded excitedly toward the group. These ridgebacks, on the other hand, had self-control; they didn't look at one another let alone the leaping young dog trying to get their attention.

The trainers began the class by explaining the basics of handling in the show ring. I'd watched my fair share of Westminster dog shows, and I honestly didn't think it looked that hard.

Piece of cake, I thought.

I watched as the ridgebacks and their owners trotted around in a circle, one-by-one. I thought they looked good, but they weren't even close to Nairobi. My pride swelled; he was *much* more talented than the other dogs! Then it was our turn. Suddenly, butterflies swirled in my stomach. My palms were sweaty. Nairobi pranced in anticipation. After a few good steps, he broke into a run, leapt happily at the other dogs sitting calmly in a circle, and jumped up to kiss me on the face, smashing his skull into my cheekbone.

Ouch!

Tears sprang to my eyes from the pain, but I kept on. I felt like an utter fool. Worse, my happy dog was completely oblivious. I was filled with shame—and appropriately mortified when I recognized that feeling.

We barely made one round of the circle before the trainer called out: "Okay, Carol! That's good for a first try. Take a rest."

We slunk back into the crowd of ridgebacks.

Next up, "stacking": this is where the dog is supposed to plant two front feet under its shoulder, extend its back legs, hold its head up—and freeze. I got Nairobi into the perfect position—four legs perfectly organized—and then he moved his front leg half an inch. I leaned down to put the foot back into place, and his back leg shifted. I put his back leg into position, and he moved his front leg. I straightened up for a moment and checked out the other dogs; they were stacked perfectly, like statues.

Oh, brother.

I leaned down again to get Nairobi into position, and in response, he turned and gave me a big wet slurp: *This is fun!*

I spent the rest of the class in a bent-over position adjusting Nairobi's legs.

WE ATTENDED THREE HANDLING CLASSES altogether, and each one was as bad as the first. I felt alternately anxious, awkward, and competitive—and absolutely silly for feeling that way. I chatted to a few of the owners after classes, and they tried to be supportive, but it was clear to everyone, including myself, that Nairobi and I were really quite awful at this.

Nairobi, for his part, thought the classes were great. He expressed his nature effortlessly: exuberant, joyful, energetic, and free of self-consciousness. And he treated every class like date night. He'd stare longingly at the female dogs in class, trying to seduce them, and puff himself up to stare down and intimidate the rival males.

Unfortunately, if he didn't learn how to stack properly, Nairobi would never get a chance with the saucy ridgeback girls. They could only mate with males making their AKC championship points. At the rate we were going, we'd be lucky to accrue a polite goodbye, let alone points. I didn't have the heart to break it to him.

WHEN IT CAME TIME FOR our first dog show, I was nervous. I tried talking some sense into myself. *This is just a dog show, Carol. There's absolutely nothing to worry about.*

It didn't work.

The only comfort was that Nairobi's ears seemed under control that day. In fact, he looked quite beautiful; his coat was glossy red, his temperament frisky and playful. I adored him and felt quite proud.

I met my breeder at the show, and she was all business, giving me last-minute instructions, and offering some insight into the dog show process. Nairobi seemed overjoyed to see so many dogs, but all I saw were dog owners sizing him up, calculating whether he would be serious competition.

Ha! Just wait until we get to stacking.

Nairobi and I entered the ring along with the other dogs and their handlers. My mind went blank. Competition of any kind affects me that way. I took a deep breath, but I caught the disapproving eye of my breeder in the crowd.

I immediately stopped breathing.

The judge directed us to trot in a circle, and we all set off in formation.

So far so good.

Without warning, Nairobi suddenly tugged hard against the leash, which snapped under the strain. There was a collective gasp as Nairobi ran playfully up to every ridgeback in the ring, greeting them with enthusiasm. The handlers were horrified, the dogs ignored Nairobi—but he was undeterred. With a crazed, wide-eyed expression, he then ran toward the horrified judge, jumped up, and planted a wet tongue kiss on her face. A few people laughed as I grabbed Nairobi's collar and dragged him out of the ring.

My face turned bright red, but I didn't have the heart to be mad at him. He was just a silly, funny dog—who made me look ridiculous. I have some pride, and I did feel uncomfortable, but I didn't miss the humor in the situation.

Get over yourself, Carol.

My breeder was kind about the incident, but I could see that she was disappointed. I was just relieved it was over—and vaguely hopeful that our failure would translate to a reprieve from the show ring.

As I drove home with Nairobi fast asleep in the back of the car, I started to frame our dog show fiasco into a story. It was funny. *Really* funny. Henry was going to love it.

"Maybe you should try agility," the trainers suggested, encouragingly over the phone. "It will help Nairobi mature."

I'd only seen agility competitions on television—those funny exhibitions on Animal Planet where dogs jump over fences, weave through poles, and race through tunnels—and the sport appeared to involve true teamwork between dog and handler. It wasn't about dominance nor was it about obedience; instead it involved working side-by-side with an animal to achieve a goal. The dogs looked like they were having a blast and, unlike the control required for show dogs, agility dogs looked, and acted, a little wild and crazy.

I liked the idea. A lot.

Agility sounded like *us*.

COME! JUMP!

The process of getting to know your dog can set off a chain reaction of personal introspection: *Who am I? What's my true character? What kinds of work, play, or people suit me? What do I stand for? What's holding me back from happiness?*

But asking the questions is a whole lot easier than answering them.

"How was the dog show?" Henry asked a few nights later while we were having a glass of wine in his kitchen—dinner simmering fragrantly on the stove. The connection between us felt liquid: warm, exciting—filled with anticipation and promise.

"Imagine this scene," I began. "We're surrounded by perfectly behaved dogs. Nairobi has his nose up, sniffing—a big dog-smile on his face. I was nervous, but I was trying to stay focused as we entered the ring—glances all around as everyone checked out the competition."

Henry's lips turned up in a small smile. He was entertained. I loved that.

"So," I continued, "the judge, a lovely, dignified woman wearing a conservative dress, pearls, and blazer, walks into the ring and tells us to proceed in a circle."

I could feel Henry's enjoyment of this story. It was a high for me, these moments when I could paint a picture that pleased him.

"We start trotting around, and Nairobi starts leaping. I try to settle him down, but I don't know, he just kept picking up speed—and snap! The leash broke and he was off!"

Henty gave a low chuckle.

"I'm chasing him like an idiot; he's whirling away from me, enjoying the attention, scampering and jumping around like a happy rabbit, and then he headed straight for the judge! He jumped up and kissed her on the face!"

There was a big smile on Henry's face.

"It was so *embarrassing*—and I felt awful for the judge. She must have been scared for a minute. But Nairobi was so pleased with his performance—he acted like he'd won best in show!"

We enjoyed a warm moment of laughter together before Henry announced with finality, "Well, that's the end of your dog show career."

"For the moment," I answered, bristling at the way he'd assumed control of my decision. His response felt like ice on my hot skin. It was one thing for me to give up hopes for Nairobi in the show ring; it was a whole other thing for Henry to proclaim it.

"But I *do* think we're going to try dog agility," I added, perhaps with a bit of challenge in my tone. "My handling trainers suggested it."

"What's agility?" Henry asked, frowning.

HENRY HAD BEEN IN MY life for five years. When we first began seeing one another, my kids were at home, and they acted as a natural buffer between Henry and me, which got us off to a slow start. Henry was not step-father potential. It's not that he wasn't a good man; he was simply finished with raising kids. In his case, he'd already raised two sons as a single father. As the primary parent for my children, I had no issue keeping a boyfriend separate from my family life. As the years went by, though, things loosened up; we traveled together, enjoyed good food, talked politics and literature—but we were two very different people. We did not share the same feelings about life or relationships. We spoke different languages when it came to emotional support and expressions of affection. We lived separately. We broke up often, then got back together, and despite the volatility in our relationship, I was committed, quite convinced of my destiny: This man and I were going to spend the rest of our lives together. I can't say the idea brought me great joy, but I loved him, believed he loved me too, and I was drawn to him like a magnet. I dreamed that we would mysteriously become happy—at some point. I believed that he and I would have our "moment"—he would need me, I would be there, and that would be that. Our bond would finally make sense—and be real.

Clearly, I hadn't thought this through very well.

But the clear-thinking phase of my life was about to begin.

NOT LONG AFTER THE DOG show debacle, I signed up for dog agility training. Two evenings a week, from six to seven o'clock, I'd make the forty-five minute drive north from my home in Santa Monica to Reseda, which is in the San Fernando Valley. Class was held on a flat, dusty field behind a multi-purpose evangelical church that leased space to the local community. Sometimes, when we were running our dogs, we could see—and hear—a belly dancing class in progress in one of the church's meeting rooms. The rhythmic shimmying of bells provided an interesting accompaniment to our equally eccentric endeavors.

The agility field was lit by spotlights, hung haphazardly on metal stands and fastened to trees. The obstacle course was made up of jumps (wooden frames on each side with horizontal poles that could be adjusted for different heights), a tire obstacle (literally, a plastic or rubber tire suspended between a metal frame), a ten-foot industrial fabric tunnel or two, weave poles (vertical wooden poles held in place by a track secured by metal stakes hammered into the ground), a pause table (a low, square table), a metal teeter (seesaw), an A-frame (two broad ramps with treads that form a steep A-shape), and a dog walk (a balance beam with ramps on both sides). The equipment was battered from contant use; whatever bright colored paint had decorated each obstacle had long disappeared.

When I arrived for my first class, there was an advanced class in progress. It was thrilling to watch, though definitely intimidating. I couldn't figure out how it all worked, but men and women were running hard through the dark, dogs were flying over jumps, grinding to a halt, turning on a dime, barking, weaving through the poles—there was a great deal of adrenaline flowing. There was also a lot of shouting as handlers bellowed, "Jump *left!* Go *right!* Come *front!*"

I looked down at Nairobi who was quivering with excitement.

I was excited, too.

And holding court over this domain was Irina.

Thin, small, intense, in her late thirties, she had a perfect oval-shaped face with delicate features. Her complexion was nut-brown from years of competing in the harsh sun. Irina was quite beautiful—but there was an austerity and focus to her that did not invite approach. She reminded me of the Catholic school nuns I knew as a kid—serious, no-nonsense women who expected to be obeyed. I was scared of them all.

Irina had the same effect on me

I never saw Irina wear make-up or jewelry, or dress in anything other than agility clothes: a puffy down jacket or vest, gray sweatpants, a black turtleneck, and her brown hair was swept off her face in a high ponytail either tucked under a wool knit cap or beneath a wide headband that covered her ears. She was always cold and even in the summer she wore turtlenecks. Swathed in head wrappings or scarves, her bare face peeked out as if from behind the veil and wimple of a nun's habit.

Irina greeted every dog with a slow, reserved smile while watching them out of the corner of her eye, assessing their personalities, their physicality, and their interactions with their owners. She seemed to grasp the whole picture in just a few seconds.

People were greeted with a polite, old-world formality, but with the same cool assessment.

Irina didn't miss a trick.

From the beginning, my classmates and I were uniformly awful. It might look easy to get a dog to step over a six-inch jump, but it's not. Many dogs just sat in front of the jump and stared curiously at it. *What the heck is this?*

"Come! Jump!" we all pleaded, holding treats in our hands. The dogs looked at us like we were insane. We begged, stumbled, dropped our dog treats, and bumped into obstacles that collapsed on contact by design so the dogs wouldn't get hurt. It was one big, noisy mess. Aside from Nairobi, most of the dogs in the class were smaller: a sheltie, a couple of mutts, a Lhasa apso, and a golden retriever.

None of us had the slightest clue that we were being taught by a world-class agility competitor—we were too busy feeling intimidated. Irina ran her classes in a no-nonsense fashion and had little patience for "badly behaved" owners, which we quickly learned meant talking to one another, asking inappropriate questions, letting dogs pull at their leashes, and speaking angrily to a dog. I once said a few kind words to a classmate about her success with an exercise, and Irina bellowed from across the field, "*Quiet!* No *talking!*"

I never did *that* again.

We progressed slowly—and quietly—waiting our turn at attempting the obstacles. The dogs remained on leash except when they were on the course. We all kept our distance from one another—literally—because in addition to Irina's "no talking" rule, there was a "stay five feet away" rule.

When Irina called out instructions, she would often turn her head away from us to look at the course, which made her inaudible. Sometimes she walked the course while talking, which made it even harder to hear her. The group of us would trot after her, ears strained to catch what she was saying—trying not to get too close to one another in the process.

"What did she say?" one of us would whisper.

"I don't know. *Shh*," another would whisper back.

"Quiet! She's looking this way!" someone else would mutter softly.

We acted like scared kids—exactly the effect Irina was going for.

OUR TREKS TO THE AGILITY field were the high points of Nairobi's week. He would get terribly excited the moment we got in the car and headed for the freeway.

Unfortunately, his exuberance soon got us into trouble.

I don't know if it was aggression, high spirits, or just Nairobi's way of breaking the tension of waiting his turn. It didn't matter. But one night, while we were standing quietly in the shadows, he lunged aggressively toward the small Shetland sheepdog. I corrected Nairobi quickly, but the woman who owned the sheltie was visibly upset.

Once my heart stopped racing from the near disaster, I ran back the event in my mind, and realized that the sheltie had been glaring at Nairobi. With a young dog's swagger, Nairobi had simply answered the challenge. Of course, the sheltie was much smaller than Nairobi, and when it comes to dogs, the bigger dog is always at fault. A big dog can simply do more harm.

While Nairobi reacted instinctually, it was my fault for letting it happen in the first place; I should have turned him away. Nothing good ever comes from two dogs staring at one another.

At the next class, the sheltie and her owner were nowhere to be found. Apparently, the woman had complained that she was afraid of my dog, so Irina had moved her to another class.

Before I began training with Irina, I wasn't as careful as I should have been with my dogs—I realize that now—but I always kept my dogs on leash and under control. And since training with Irina, I have become a vigilant dog owner. I have come to realize that dogs . . . are *dogs*. Sometimes they fight, get aggressive, and behave in an obstreperous fashion. I know my dogs are a handful and I warn strangers who come near. "Are they friendly?" Not always. "Can I pet them?" No.

So, the woman and her troublemaking sheltie had a point. I spent a few guilty nights worrying about this issue, and I came to the conclusion that I had chosen a big, complicated dog and I was responsible for him—and for everyone who might come into contact with him. The dog that sleeps in your lap and gazes at you with loving, sweet eyes—though it may be hard to believe —is also capable of attacking when provoked . . . or sometimes, just for fun. Some dogs enjoy a little dustup.

So do some people.

In my relationship with Henry, I'd say he was the provocative sheltie and I was the easily baited Nairobi. After an argument, I would run through the scene in my mind and discover that my frustration with Henry could always be traced back to the people version of a dog stare-down.

I always answered the challenge.

AFTER THE SHELTIE INCIDENT, IRINA encouraged me to move Nairobi into a private class during the day. She felt it would be a good idea to have our learning take place without the distraction of other dogs— especially the smaller ones, which seemed so adept at getting Nairobi riled up.

Every Monday afternoon from one to two o'clock, Nairobi and I turned up for class with Irina. It was fun playing with Nairobi, and he was eager to learn. We spent the first few months progressing slowly and steadily. Even though Irina would occasionally fly off the handle with a loud reprimand when I made I mistake, I looked forward to our sessions. Irina was getting to know us, and more importantly, she was gauging my seriousness in the sport. The fact that I was committed to excelling at agility meant a lot to her, and we began to develop a broader relationship that encompassed our personal lives. During breaks in training, while Nairobi rested, Irina and I would talk. She told me about her former career as a graphic designer in Germany where she lived with her musician boyfriend; she regaled me with tales of her world travels, and her decision to move to Los Angeles to concentrate on dog agility. I shared stories about my advertising agency, the novel I was working on, details about my sons, my family—and Henry.

At first, I just painted a picture for her. Henry was older, successful, and brilliant. As time went by, I was more frank. Henry was complicated and critical. I usually found myself on the defensive with him. He wasn't enthusiastic about life—or me. I often felt like my optimism was being dashed by the pitcher of cold water that was Henry.

Yes, I loved him. At that point, I assumed that most of our arguments were my fault, because I was the one who was usually mad. I was committed to practicing patience, though, because I was very attached to him, but my frustration would build up and there we'd be—in a dustup.

Irina was a very good listener—until she had something to say. Once her thoughts on an issue codified in her mind, she would launch off on a lengthy explanation of her opinion on the matter—*any* matter. But while she was listening, her head cocked slightly, she would become very still and look off into the distance, thinking. When she was gathering information, she asked a lot of questions, completely without judgment. I never really knew what Irina thought about anything I said until she was a few minutes into one of her teaching monologues.

One day, I showed up to class in a bad mood. Irina took one look at my face and asked me what was wrong.

"Oh, it's Henry. I'm so frustrated with him."

Irina gave me a "go on" look.

"We went to my friend Peter's party at the beach. It was really fun. I saw people I hadn't seen in ages, I was making some business contacts, I introduced Henry to a bunch of people, and we'd just been there for an hour and he made a face at me across the room and pointed to his watch."

Irina asked, "What did you do?"

"Well, I dragged my feet for fifteen minutes, and then I left with him."

Irina took a moment to think. "When you've gone to these parties in the past, did you make a big fuss and act pleased when he went?"

"No," I answered.

"Do you have fun with him at these parties?"

"Not at *my* friends' parties. He's usually difficult and moody. When he has a party, and people he knows are around, we have fun."

"Ah, so he likes to *give* parties," Irina said.

"He does."

"Well, if he isn't getting anything positive out of going to your friends' parties, why would he go?"

"To be nice to me?"

Irina considered my response and then asked, "Is Henry ever just nice to you for no reason?"

I paused. I honestly had to think about this. While Henry was certainly capable of being nice, he was not, by nature, *nice*. He was a rather grumpy, self-absorbed man. That's not to say I couldn't get him to laugh at my bad jokes and listen to my long-winded stories, but his agreeableness had more to do with how comfortable *he* felt in a situation than anything to do with me. He was not the guy who put gas in my car or brought me coffee. I honestly hadn't cared very much about this issue. I was used to it. But I had never articulated it. Henry had many fine qualities; he was interesting, even charming, and even though he didn't lead with the kindness card—or even have it in his deck—he was a responsible man who fulfilled his obligations.

"No," I finally said.

"So, he isn't a man brimming with love and goodwill?"

I didn't even have to think before answering, "No, he isn't."

"Well, he sounds like a guy who needs a reward to be good. He needs an incentive to be cooperative and nice to you. If you want someone who's naturally easygoing and cooperative, you'll have to find another guy."

Irina's response was a complete surprise to me. *Have a man in your life who isn't nice? Try rewarding his good behavior! Or find a nice guy!*

It sounded rather silly. I mean, who stays with a guy who isn't nice?

I guess I do.

Irina was on a roll, and throughout class, she continued to emphasize her point.

"If you own a basset hound, you can't expect him to jump high jumps," she called out. "Bassett hounds are short dogs, with short legs. If you want a dog to take high jumps, you need a border collie."

"I get it, Irina."

"Asking a basset hound to act like a border collie isn't fair."

"I get it."

"You have to know your dog. If you ask too much of him, you'll both just get frustrated."

I get it, Irina. Henry is a basset hound.

KNOWING YOUR DOG MEANS understanding his capabilities. When I removed Nairobi from the show ring, it reflected knowledge of his personality, and my own. Taking him out of the group agility class showed respect for his limitations, and worked both to eliminate the possibility of trouble and increase our chances of a happy experience.

Knowing your significant other should mean the same: respecting limitations and working within what that person is truly capable of—not what you might want the person to be. Henry was always Henry-like. From the first moment I met him, he'd been consistent. Yet here I was, yearning for more, dreaming of a border collie man, fun-loving and up for an adventure. I was in a relationship with a basset hound, and if I wanted some kind of happiness with him, I'd just have to work with those short legs, enjoy the velvety ears, and cut our walks a bit shorter.

But what was I doing in a relationship with a basset hound in the first place? I wasn't quite sure what kind of a dog I was, but I was pretty sure I wasn't a basset hound. I was an enthusiastic, high-spirited woman partnered with an ill-tempered, low-energy man. It occurred to me that I might be the problem here.

How could I have missed this basic truth?

Because I am not a dog.

Have a Cookie

chapter two

When it comes to dogs, rewards are much
more effective than demands,
and a yes is always better than a no.
From there, it's just a small step to
realizing that it's the same for all of us.

When I started agility, the first lesson I learned was to treat my dogs with "cookies" after every effort. Just to be clear, a "cookie" is the term Irina used to refer to any kind of a treat; the juicier the better—and it was always reinforced by Irina's training clicker.

Take a jump—get a cookie. *Click.*

Go through the weave poles—get a cookie. *Click.*

Sit, stay . . . get a cookie. *Click.*

I have to say, this seemed a bit tedious. Why couldn't my dog simply do what I told him without being rewarded?

One day early in my training I was running a course with Nairobi and we seemed to be doing well. Nairobi was alert and responsive, watching me for direction. I called him over the first jump, and he cleared the twenty-four inches with room to spare, then he took the second jump, and it was off to the tunnel—where he could disappear into the darkness for a few seconds, playing hide-and-seek with me. Nairobi loved dashing through the tunnel, and he always burst out the other end searching for my face with a dopey expression of joy on his. Then it was on to the weave poles, which were more of a challenge. To teach the dog to "weave" around each one, like a race car around orange cones, took patience. You have to walk the dog through while holding the collar, offering treats, and basically keep this up until the dog can do it on its own. And here we were, in a good rhythm, about to hit the poles. Dog agility requires the handler to be just as focused and directed as the dog, and instead of concentrating on the weave poles, my mind leapt forward to the jump we were supposed to take next. My hand loosed on Nairobi's collar, and he simply wandered away. There I was, bent over the poles all by myself. It felt like I'd been stood-up at the altar.

"*Hey!*" I yelled. "Nairobi! *Come!*"

Nairobi returned to my side with a sheepish look on his face.

Then very purposefully, Irina got out of her folding chair and walked slowly in my direction.

Uh-oh.

She stood close to me, staring somewhere over my shoulder, eyes squinted in thought.

There was a long moment of silence before she asked, "Do you work for free?"

I had become used to her trick questions and, honestly, at that point in our training I was wary of her occasional bursts of temper so I answered carefully. "Uh . . . I don't think so."

"You get money for your work, right?"

"Right," I answered more confidently.

"Then why do you expect Robi to work for you when you aren't paying him?"

I thought about this for a moment. "How do I pay him?"

"With cookies."

Ah-ha! Cookies!

"You forgot to treat him. You should have given him a cookie after the first two jumps before sending him into the tunnel."

"Right."

"That's his paycheck. Cookies are his salary. He doesn't work for free."

"Got it."

"And when Robi gets his cookies, he's happy, and then he'll work harder and see the work as fun. When he gets a reward, work becomes a game. And when agility becomes a game, anything is possible."

If you're going to ask a dog to take high jumps, scoot through tunnels, and maneuver through narrow weave poles, you'd better have something tasty for him on the other end. That day, I had raw hot dogs in my sticky hands, and as we ran the course again, I treated Robi liberally and, though he barely paused to snatch his morsel of hot dog from my hand, he seemed to jump higher, run faster, and generally work harder with increased enjoyment. At the end of the course, he barreled toward me, jumped up, and licked my face enthusiastically.

When an eighty-pound Rhodesian ridgeback is happy, you feel it. Evidently, Robi loved getting paid.

Irina explained that rewarding effort, whether it was successful or not, increased the dog's enjoyment and kept the work they were doing associated with pleasure. And then she asked me why I wouldn't want to make their work pleasurable? It was a simple question that stuck in my mind.

"When you were raising your children," Irina asked, "didn't you get excited about *everything* that was new for them? Every time they ate a new food, or the first time they smiled, or took their first step? Didn't you get enthusiastic about every new experience?"

Wow.

I thought back to everything I had exposed my children to for the first time—whether it was eating lima beans or going for a ride on the Ferris wheel—and there I was with a happy smile on my face and encouraging words. When did I stop doing that?

Why did I stop doing that?

Life had become a series of expectations and demands. Whether dealing with myself and my work, or dealing with my kids, friends, and coworkers, rewarding good behavior certainly got me a lot further than demanding good behavior. Kindness to myself and to those around me elicited better responses than demands.

I tried this out on myself first and found that changing my thought process a bit to acknowledging my efforts instead of focusing on my deficits worked wonders with my attitude. At the end of each work day, I made a point to congratulate myself on what I'd accomplished instead of focusing on the tasks I hadn't yet completed. It was a subtle adjustment, but it made a big difference.

Then I tried it out in the real world.

The telephone repairman responded warmly—and industriously—to kind conversation instead of complaints about my phone service.

Vendors I worked with at my ad agency readily responded to "thanks for being timely" and "I appreciate your efforts."

My handyman, Wilfredo, responded too. He responded even more enthusiastically to better tips.

My kids were delighted when I heaped praise on them for helping me bring in the groceries or set the table; it made them offer to do more chores around the house—an unexpected benefit.

My neighbors responded to my kindly worded requests.

When I tried out the reward system on Henry, however, it failed. He lapped up the praise, appreciation, and affection, but there didn't seem to be any lasting effect from my efforts. "You look so handsome!" made him glow for a minute and then it was back to the business of being Henry.

One night, Henry sat across from me at the dinner table, tapping his fingers on the table. He'd finished eating, but I was only half done.

"You are such a wonderful cook! I just love this chicken!" I said, taking another bite.

Henry gave me a quick, close-mouthed smile, and then his craggy face fell serious. "I think it had too much salt," he said.

"Oh, *I* don't. I thought it was perfect! Thank you so much!"

"You liked it?" he asked.

"Very much. You are an *amazing* cook."

"Thanks."

He seemed quite happy for a few seconds. His green eyes focused on me and I smiled. I poured a little more wine in his glass, and started to take a sip of my own, getting ready to continue our conversation and keep the happy feelings going when Henry suddenly stood up saying, "I'm going to get started on the dishes." As he left the room he called over his shoulder, "Don't forget to clear the table."

Ha!

I sat alone, finishing my dinner, picturing him furiously scrubbing the dishes that I would have gladly washed—but Henry didn't like the way I handled his pots and pans.

Henry entirely disproved the logic behind the reward versus the demand system. He liked the rewards. He noticed kind behavior from me and always commented on it; it just didn't obligate him to be nice in return. It was a dilemma.

Despite what I was getting in return, I decided to continue with the grateful attitude. Time would tell whether it would ultimately change anything, but I certainly liked myself a whole lot better.

TAKE SMALL BITES

The reward system with dogs is based on degree of effort. At the beginning of training, every attempt is treated with a cookie. Every effort is treated with a cookie. Take a jump, get a reward. Don't take the jump, but look like you might want to? Get a cookie.

Before a dog can jump two jumps, he has to jump one. Before he can bound over the A-frame, he actually has to step on the A-frame. And for every effort and stage in this process, the dog is getting treats and praise. It shows the dog that one step is as good as two, and three steps are as good as four. Before the dog knows it, he's learned something new. It's almost effortless.

This approach to teaching dogs new exercises is slow. Weeks of treating for baby steps on the dog walk can seem laborious, but what a surprise when after a month or so, your dog actually takes the obstacle without stopping. And what a miracle when after a year, your dog is running over it and you can hardly keep up.

Breaking training into small bite-sized pieces removes the pressure from achieving an ultimate goal, which can prove daunting sometimes.

And if something goes wrong in the training process, you've learned the technique to fix it.

Nairobi is always fearless with the jumps, but he is entirely suspicious of the "teeter." Like a child's playground seesaw, an agility teeter consists of a non-skid surface plank on a fulcrum. The dog walks up the lowered side of the plank until reaching the pivot point. The dog's weight then shifts the plank's direction and he walks down the other side. The teeter is about twelve feet long, fairly narrow, but balanced equally so that even small dogs can change the pivot. Some dogs get stuck in the middle, the plank swinging in either direction, which can either be scary or a lot of fun depending on the dog. Some dogs scamper over this obstacle easily, and even enjoy banging the plank down on the other side.

When training a dog on this obstacle, treats are placed in a trail along the plank so that the dog gets lots of reinforcement. Handlers hold the dog's collar to steady the accent, and also to catch and cushion the plank as it shifts downward so that the dog isn't frightened by the sound of the plank hitting the ground.

Early in our training, we were in a night class and the field was lit up by flood lights. Nairobi had gone over the teeter several times without incident. It was the last obstacle after a series of jumps. The final time we attempted it, he was a bit too excited and he jauntily launched onto the plank from the side instead of stepping onto it from the front. Even though I'd grabbed his collar on approach, he suddenly lost his balance—and his confidence—and he jumped/fell off, the teeter banging loudly behind him. He scampered away, tail curled under his rump, ears flattened back in fear.

"*Nairobi!*" I yelled in a worried tone. "You okay?" I cooed sympathetically as I ran to him. "Aww, *sweetie.*" One look at his face and I knew he was spooked. The dark shadows around the teeter probably didn't help much, and my emotional response to his fall most likely contributed to his anxiety. Irina always tells me not to react to a mistake so as not to reinforce the dog's negative experience, but it was early on in my training and I was just too high-strung to stay calm.

As for Irina, she did *not* overreact. She eyed Nairobi quickly and asked me to trot him around so she could check his gait for injuries.

She watched closely as I jogged alongside him in a circle. "He looks fine," she said quietly. "Take him for a walk at the other end of the field."

From that moment on, Nairobi wouldn't go near that obstacle. We would take jump after jump, go through the weave poles, but then the moment he was confronted with the teeter, Nairobi's head would lower, he'd look at me with a "help me!" expression, and simply stop.

When you've made a mistake with a dog, you have to start all over again at the beginning. So, I began treating him for simply getting near the teeter. Once that was okay, he got a treat when he stepped on the teeter, and then he got treated when he took two steps. Then he'd get a treat for three steps.

Once something bad has happened with a dog, it takes time and patience to reverse the damage. It can take months. Sometimes even years.

It's the same with people.

It's taken me years to forget bad things that have happened to me in the past. Everything from embarrassments in my youth to my divorce, each painful event in my life stayed with me far too long. Some memories are hard to shake. All around me, I see people still struggling to make peace with things that happened when they were children.

Take Henry.

There were certainly many things in Henry's childhood that

might have contributed to his dark, critical outlook on life, but despite the fact that his adult life had unfolded quite easily, his early personal hurts were as fresh in his mind as if they had happened yesterday.

Henry was like Nairobi and the teeter. Somewhere along the way, Henry had fallen off the teeter and just couldn't get back on. It could have been something as simple as falling off of a bike as a child. Each one of us has different sensitivities to emotional—and physical—hurts. Whatever the reason, it had left Henry with an inability to take a risk—to believe in love. He didn't trust that the weight of his being, his own love, could change the pivot, and bring him down safely on the other side.

So I continued with my positive reinforcement and hoped that, someday, Henry would run toward the teeter (me) and lick my face happily.

BREAKING TASKS INTO SMALL PIECES was extremely valuable in my professional life. I had a small advertising agency and the last project I worked on with my freelance art director, Sarah, was a complicated one. She and I had a thorny relationship, mostly based on the natural miscommunication to be found between writers (verbal communicators) and art directors (visual communicators). We'd worked together off and on for close to seven years, and while the end results were always worth the friction between us, I still found the process difficult. I began each project by explaining the big picture, outlining the parameters of the project, and sharing visual references. Our first meetings were always terrific. Somewhere between our initial discussions and Sarah's delivery of her work, she would execute explorations way beyond the scope of our conversation. She would turn up with twenty, sometimes thirty design options for me, which I found overwhelming. For her part, since I billed my clients when assignments were completed, Sarah had to wait for her invoices to be paid, which can be typical for a freelancer, but it was frustrating for her. Her professional background was at a large ad agency, and she was used to getting a weekly paycheck. Since breaking tasks into small pieces was working so well for me, I decided to try the strategy with Sarah.

For the first assignment of developing a logo, I decided to limit the time for her to deliver her design work. Her best designs were typically her first few, so I thought the shortened timeframe might limit her output. I gave Sarah five days and asked her to do what she could in that time frame. She was frantic. "I can't possibly design a logo in five days!"

I reassured her. "Don't worry about what you design. Just do what you can do. It'll be fine."

Instead of getting twenty layouts, I received three focused designs to choose from. And they were fabulous.

We went on to work on several more design elements for the client, and instead of paying her fee at the entire project's completion, I advanced her a weekly check. The results were fantastic. She was pleased to have money in her pocket, happy that I was so satisfied with her work, and we both had a sense of completion at each step in the process.

Bite-size pieces of work plus rewards, rewards, rewards . . . it worked.

I was so excited about how well the technique had worked with my art director, I happily relayed the story to Irina.

She smiled as she listened.

"You had to work *that* hard to get her to produce what you wanted?"

"Yes."

"And you've worked with her for seven years?"

"Yes."

"And you pay her well?"

"It's the standard rate."

"Is she a good art director?"

"She is."

"But there are a lot of good art directors around, right?"

I nodded. "Sure."

Irina looked at me and shook her head. "You should have fired her years ago."

JUMP, COME, COOKIE

Once I learned to reward every effort from my dogs, Irina taught me how to build a sequence, so that up to three actions were required to get a reward. The "jump, come, cookie" sequence is my favorite because Nairobi seems to enjoy it so much. The sequence is rather simple: Nairobi sits by my side facing a jump, I send him over it, he answers to my "come" call by returning and sitting in front of me, and I reward him with a cookie.

Nairobi enjoyed this game immensely.

As training progressed, he even learned to jump "right" and jump "left." It was remarkable to me that a dog could learn to jump in a certain direction.

I wasn't quite sure why Nairobi liked the "jump, come, cookie" sequence so much, but he would do it over and over wearing an expression of pure joy. Perhaps it simply combined his two favorite activities: jumping and eating. It might also have been the instant gratification offered by the exercise. Whatever the reason, he loved it so much that sometimes while walking on or off of the field he would break away from my side, spontaneously take the nearest jump, and rush back to me for a cookie.

"Carol!" Irina would yell. "Don't let Nairobi take an obstacle by himself. That's dangerous!"

Oops.

I'd grab Robi and put him back on the leash, but his tail would be wagging happily. I think he just loved the idea that getting a cookie was this simple.

I TOOK A CUE FROM THIS exercise and applied it to myself. Since I was often working on more than one project at a time, I began to break my work into smaller segments: two hours on one project, two hours on another, a half hour break, an hour for the gym, back for two hours of work, dinner break, then back to work. After every segment, I rewarded myself with a "good effort" thought, and proceeded to the next.

Viewing my work day as a series of completed sequences increased my creative output tremendously. It also decreased my anxiety. In the past, I would start my day with a vague list of all the things I had to do as well as find time for my writing. Some days, I would get so overwhelmed by the sheer amount of work, I'd stare in a daze in front of the computer, or call a friend and chat instead. Setting a finite amount of time for each task gave me a sense of a beginning and an end. It relieved stress and allowed me to accomplish more and to receive satisfaction when a work segment was completed.

Seeing a relationship as a series of finite sequences also brings a shift in attitude. With Henry, this process worked to help me enjoy the fun times we had together. A cozy lunch, a good conversation, a sweet smile—they were small things, but they added up. Sometimes a disagreement in the morning could merge into a tense conversation in the evening, and could still be found in my irritable mood the following morning. When I tried to separate my life with Henry into sequences—some good, some not so—it helped me achieve some balance with him.

Jump, come, cookie is a kind of philosophy based on efforts and rewards. It's a simple way to train a dog, and it's a good way to move through life. There's a natural flow to it, and when you practice it, it builds confidence. I realized that rewards for my efforts didn't have to come from the outside; I was perfectly capable of cheering myself on.

* * *

NEVER SAY NO

In class, I watched Irina correct dogs with an "oops" or a "wrong," or sometimes she wouldn't say anything to the dog and just move him back to the starting line to try again.

Irina never says "no."

While this may seem like a simple concept, I discovered many things about my dogs and myself by removing "no" from my vocabulary. My dogs immediately stopped acting sheepish or guilty and were more enthusiastic in their willingness to keep trying to achieve the goals I had set for them.

It may be hard for some people to believe that dogs actually feel guilty, but if you've ever seen a dog get yelled at or corrected in an angry tone, you've seen the energy seep right out of him like a balloon being deflated. And conversely, when a dog senses approval, he will go over jump after jump with complete enthusiasm. If you want a dog to keep giving you his best effort, you need his energy to be positive. And that means *your* energy needs to stay positive. Correcting my dogs with an "oops" took the emotion out of me, and therefore I didn't communicate that negative emotion to them.

All frustration with my dogs and their behavior simply disappeared. There were no more ugly emotional scenes or frustrating tugs of war. When they made a mistake, I didn't refer to it and began the exercise again, or I made a neutral correction like "wrong" and we went back to the starting line.

The transformation in my relationship with my dogs, and even my feelings about them, changed the very moment I stopped saying "no." The power of that simple word wasn't lost on me, and each week as I drove home from class with the dogs asleep in the back of my car, I explored applying that principle to myself.

I had developed the bad habit of self-criticism. Even calling myself an idiot when I'd made an error on something had become increasingly common. I started to be aware of all the "no's" I was saying to myself. I banged my head on the kitchen cabinet one morning and my mind formed the words *what a dope* instead of *ouch*. It wasn't pretty. I stopped it immediately.

When a work interaction didn't go as planned, I said "oops," and moved on.

When a day working on my novel produced only one bad paragraph, I made a decision to take a break and go back to the starting line the next day.

By curbing anger at myself, I was suddenly filled with an ongoing source of positive creative energy. My workflow improved, my moods were stable, and I did, actually, become more creative because I wasn't limiting my output to what was correct; I was just focused on my output.

Eliminating the "no" habit took the negative drama out of everyday living. I applied it everywhere in my life. If I found myself eating a chocolate when I'd sworn off chocolate, I just said "oh well" and made an agreement with myself to try harder. If I responded in a negative way to criticism or was rude to someone during the day, I used consciousness to examine the issue, acknowledged the incident with a "wrong," and started all over again. The sheer accumulation of negative feelings that had been my former style was replaced by a more humble, more aware, more positive me.

This didn't happen immediately. Self-criticism is a hard habit to break. And when you're invested in doing the right thing, it's even more of a challenge. One of my very big flaws is my work style. When I'm writing, I am so focused, so engaged in my mind, I barely notice if someone has walked into the room. Henry found this infuriating. One day, when he arrived at my house, I called "hi" over my shoulder and didn't stop working and get up to greet him. Later, over dinner, he told me how hurt he felt when I'd ignored him. I immediately launched into an internal monologue of self-reproach. *That was so stupid! How could I have been so rude? I'm so thoughtless!* And then I caught myself.

"I'm so sorry for that. I get so absorbed when I'm working, but I'll work on it. I promise."

And I moved on.

For me, the word "no" began to define a choice—not a self-correction. It's a powerful word in the right circumstances, but it's not used as a weapon against myself, my dogs, or those I love.

And in my examination of this complex word that has so much negative emotion attached to it, I rediscovered another amazing word that I'd almost forgotten: yes.

Go!

chapter three

Moving forward is necessary
in dog agility—and in life.

Just watch where you're going.

I n agility, the "go" command sends the dog ahead of you to an obstacle. When a dog has been trained to walk or work beside you, it can feel strange to be suddenly released into the unknown. Some dogs take off like rabbits, happy to be free. Others hang back, glancing back at you over their shoulder, unsure.

In life, a "yes" means "go." And like dogs, it can feel strange to be released into the unknown. As adults, all we have to guide us is instinct, information we have at the time, and blind faith. But unlike with agility, in life there is no one calling out commands behind us, steering us in the right direction.

WHEN MY CHILDREN WERE YOUNG, we moved to Southern California from New York City, and we rented a house with a pool. This is rather normal for many California homes, but to my sons and me, it was paradise. And with every pool comes a pool man. Our pool man, Jed, turned up one day with an Australian shepherd puppy in his arms, which he promptly transferred into mine.

"She needs a good home," Jed said.

The bundle of fur squirmed in my arms and looked up at me with trusting brown eyes. The kiss on my cheek sealed the deal.

"Will you take her?" Jed asked.

I didn't even think. "Yes."

It was February 13, and I decided that this puppy would be a Valentine's Day gift to my boys. I don't know how I accomplished it, but I hid that whining puppy from my curious seven and three-year-old sons for an entire day and night. On Valentine's Day morning, they burst into my bedroom at six-thirty in the morning, as was their custom, and both of them noticed the playpen I'd pulled out of the garage and placed beside my bed.

"What's *that*, Mom?"

"It's our new puppy! Happy Valentine's Day!"

"Aww!" they squealed as they ran to the playpen, scooping up the puppy into their arms—lovestruck.

We named her Cana; our miracle.

She was also wild, fearless, and as she grew, I think she considered us lost sheep in need of herding. She nipped at our ankles, nudged us, circled the boys to force them in a direction—usually away from the pool—and generally felt that she needed to guide the entire household. To tell the truth, we needed some direction at the time, and in her way, Cana filled the position. She ran fast and died too young, but she was our shepherd during tough times.

MY FIRST BOYFRIEND AFTER my divorce, David, surprised the boys and me with a black Labrador retriever. When he asked me if I would accept his gift, I said, "Yes!" Where Cana had been fearless and a bit crazy, Samantha was a home girl, content to play ball with the boys, chase them while they skateboarded, and cuddle with them in front of the television. She was a good, steady soul.

But she did have her eccentricities. Other than David, Samantha was quite suspicious of men, especially men in hats. Our gardener, George, used to wear a wide-brimmed hat, and Samantha would explode into ferocious barking every time she spotted him. I had a friend, Bernie, who always wore a baseball cap, and when Samantha would see him from a distance, she would bare her teeth and scare him off.

"What's with that damn dog?" Bernie would complain.

Beats me.

Samantha also didn't like Christmas trees. From her first Christmas with us as a puppy, she'd launch herself at the tree, growling furiously. On our second Christmas with her, she brought the tree down. I discovered her hiding in my room with pieces of shattered red bulbs and silver tinsel in her fur.

One morning, driving to my office through the Beverly Hills canyon where we lived at the time, I encountered bumper-to-bumper traffic, which was unusual. As I made my way down the narrow canyon road, I saw what the trouble was. A young female dog had positioned herself in the middle of the street and was approaching each car, as if looking for someone. As I drove nearer, I could see the nervous expression on her face as she approached each car, peering in as if expecting to discover someone familiar. Without thinking, I stopped my car and got out. "Hi, sweetie," I said. "You okay?"

She looked at me and walked in my direction. The expression on her face was shy, expectant—needy. She was a slim, elegant dog, with a long pointed snout and brown and black coloring.

I opened the back door of my car.

Are you looking for me?

She hopped right in. I took that as a yes.

I called the office, cancelled my appointments, and drove straight to the vet. I had her checked out; she got her shots, and I drove her home, where she and Samantha became fast friends.

My boys were delighted. Another dog!

We named her Zoe.

When Samantha passed on, we found our first ridgeback, Blue, who was the love of my life. And Blue paved the way for Nairobi, and then to Sheila. Zoe was there through it all.

I said yes to every dog who came my way.

IN MY ROMANTIC RELATIONSHIPS, I was more practiced at saying no. Having failed at marriage, I'd say I was doubtful of my ability
to find the right man and develop the kind of relationship that would
make a good marriage. The problem was that I was attracted to difficult
men; they were a puzzle I felt compelled to solve.

Henry was a perfect example. But even though our relationship
was emotionally charged, and quite awful at times, we had some truly
hilarious moments together.

One of my strategies to lighten Henry's frequent bad moods was
to put on a show. I play the fool quite well, and I'm a pretty good
mimic, so any encounters Henry had with interesting or eccentric people was cause for entertainment, particularly for me. I have an acute
appreciation of the absurd. The counterpoint between steadfast, dead-
pan, predictable Henry—and the world—was often hysterical.

We were staying in a rather formal hotel in Asalo, Italy, one June,
and the concierge—a tall, handsome, overweight man with heavily-
accented English and a florid complexion—became the unintended
star of our trip. He wore a morning coat every day, which was too snug
for his robust frame, and his earnest enthusiasm and red-faced cheer-
fulness was a huge contrast to Henry's demeanor, which was generally
skeptical and always sensitive to any perceived slight.

Dressed in a beautiful blue suit and white collared shirt unbut-
toned at the neck, Henry approached the front desk on our first morning at the hotel. He liked to dress up in Europe. I called him "Prada
Man" when we travelled.

"Bon *journo!*" the concierge said brightly.

"*Bon journo,*" Henry replied slowly, and loudly. He always thought that sound amplification solved all language barriers. "Do you have a *converter?*" Henry asked, miming plugging something into an electrical socket. The concierge watched, fascinated, eyebrows raised.

The concierge's face finally lit up with excitement. "*Ah,* I *see!*" he exclaimed enthusiastically. "For your *phone?* The . . . *electricity!* The current is not the same, *yes?*"

"Yes," Henry answered.

"We have *many* requests for this, you see. The guests, they forget these things, and then, the mobile phones, they do not *work!*" The concierge let out a cheery laugh.

"Right," Henry said. "Do you have one?"

The concierge tilted his head, thinking. "I do not have that information at this moment, but I will ask my *colleague.* My colleague will know. I must confer with him. I will call you in your room? After I speak with my colleague? My *colleague* is sure to have the answer!"

"Okay, call the room when you have it," Henry said glumly, and we walked to the elevator.

The moment the door shut, I could feel Henry's tension. He couldn't stand disappointment of any kind.

"Henry, about our lunch," I said. "I'm not sure."

Henry looked at me quizzically.

"I think I should confer with my *colleague.*"

Henry started to laugh quietly.

The day passed and still no sign of the converter. So Henry called down to the front desk.

"Hello!" Henry said loudly into the phone. "Have you found the converter?"

"Ah, *yes!*" I could hear the concierge's loud voice blaring through the reciver. "But *no!* I have not yet been able to reach my *colleague!* It's *terrible!* I am so *sorry* to inconvenience you!"

"Well," Henry answered in a hesitant tone. "When exactly will you be speaking to your colleague? Could you . . . could you reach your *colleague* by *telephone?*"

At that, I cracked up, then Henry followed, and the two of us could not stop laughing.

Eventually, the concierge produced a converter, but every question we asked him after that was deferred to future conversations with his mysterious colleague, which was a sign for Henry and me to start howling.

The concierge thought we were a very happy couple.

Later on that same trip, we were in Venice in a gorgeous hotel fit for a princess. Henry was in a particularly irritable mood, mostly because I had been working on my novel for two or three hours a day. He liked me to be available, and, though he tried to be patient, it was wearing on him. I decided to cheer him up.

"*Ciao*, A*dol*pho!" I greeted him as he returned from his morning walk.

"What do you mean?"

"It's so *terrible*," I went on in my best Italian accent, "because

I am a *principessa,* but a very *poor* one. I simply cannot marry you—the man I *love!*"

Henry smiled.

"My mam*ma* insists I marry the *principe* because he is rich and can save our castle, but! He is old and *ugly*, and he does not have my heart! But even though you are a poor stable boy, I far prefer *you!*"

Henry shone like a lamp switched on in a pitch black room.

"It's *terrible* this situation. I am the only one who can save my *famiglia*—and I even have to *sleep* with the *milkman* to get milk for my baby brother!"

Henry laughed.

"And the *butcher! Ah!* What *trouble!* I have to sleep with *him* for a little chicken so we can eat!"

He howled with laughter.

"But all through these *terrible* trials I think of *you*, Adolpho! I *swear!* I *adore* you!"

"And I, *principessa*, adore *you!*" Henry joined in, his face glowing.

The *"principessa"* and the stable boy skit lasted throughout our sojourn in Italy. We got such a kick out of this, and when in doubt—and usually after our second Negroni—we summoned our "colleague" for even more laughter.

WHILE MOST OF OUR ENJOYABLE times happened on vacations, which we took once a year, at home I could often lighten the atmosphere by clowning around. I would turn on the music loudly, leap around the house, yelling "time to *dance!*" Or we'd try yoga positions in the living room, which was a sight. The grimaces on Henry's face were priceless. Whenever I took control of a situation in a humorous way, Henry would join right in. One Sunday morning while Henry was making an omelet alone in the kitchen, I discovered him dancing quite merrily in his white terry cloth robe. It was so unlike him, I almost cried.

AFTER YEARS OF AGILITY WITH Nairobi, the arrival of Sheila into our home, and taking care of a now aging Zoe, I had gotten into the habit of saying yes. As for life with Henry, the emotional stability of our relationship was built entirely on my ability to humor him and keep the energy between us positive. When my will failed, we broke up—but it never lasted. I realized that I wasn't going anywhere; I was rooted to this man.

So, when he said to me casually one day, "We should get married," I said yes.

It was more of an acceptance of reality than a "yes!" I wasn't sure I was making the right decision. I may have even been positive it was the wrong decision. I just made it.

Henry said he didn't want to choose the ring alone. I'd been engaged before and had always been surprised by a ring, but Henry was insistent, so we shopped for it together. We decided on a ring that I liked, one that was in his budget. I left the purchase in his hands and hoped he'd do something romantic for the proposal.

One day soon after, Henry called me excitedly from a jewelry store.

"I found it," he said.

"Okay. What did you find?"

"A yellow diamond."

"You don't want to get the one we picked out?"

"No," Henry said. "This one is better."

My heart skipped. It wasn't that the ring wasn't beautiful; Henry emailed me a picture and it was gorgeous. It was just that Henry had a way of doing things that suited him before I got a chance to have them suit me. It was a small detail, but one I keenly felt.

He arrived home with his shopping bag, happy as I'd ever seen him, and unceremoniously gave me the ring. He watched my face closely as I opened the box.

"It's *beautiful*, Henry," I said as I kissed him.

"Put it on," he said.

I did, and he admired it.

"It looks good on you."

It did look good on my hand. I wondered, though, did Henry want me to have this ring because it looked good for *him*?

"Well, that's that," Henry said.

He went back to the office and I went back to work, periodically glancing at the bright yellow ring on my finger.

SPORTING MY GORGEOUS YELLOW DIAMOND, I turned up for agility class with Nairobi—and Sheila, who had just turned a year old.

She sat in the driver's seat of my car, anxiously watching the action. I couldn't take Zoe to agility because she barked in protest from the moment she arrived at the field.

"I got engaged!" I told Irina.

She eyed the ring and smiled. "Beautiful."

"I think it's stunning," I said, quite certain of its beauty, but not quite certain how I felt about the ring itself.

"So," Irina said. "Now, you should be happy."

There was a slight smirk on her face. *Was she being serious? Supportive? Or was she laughing at me?*

But leave it to Irina to bring up the one thing I hadn't even considered.

Happiness.

Real Time

chapter four

Dogs are in real time.
They're incapable of being anywhere else.

When people stay in real time, we experience each
moment as it comes to us. Some are amazing,
some quite painful, but each has the potential
to teach us something we need to know.

When I put Nairobi and Sheila in a "stay," and they look up at me intently waiting for their treat, they are totally, completely absorbed with the now.

If I seem angry or moody, they retreat to their kennels.

If I open the refrigerator door, they scamper into the kitchen to see what's up.

If I've left a dinner plate close to the edge of the counter and the coast is clear, both of them will jump on the counter to lick up the leftovers.

If I've stepped on their toes, they yelp in pain, and the next moment they give me kisses—the pain forgotten.

If they are on the agility field taking a jump and see a squirrel running across the field, they make a split second decision about whether to take chase or to stay and work.

And if one of them has chased the squirrel and been put back in the car for a time out, the tail is wagging when I come back to get them after ten minutes. *Hi! Nice to see you!*

Real time.

It would be amazing if we all lived there.

It's equally amazing how often I forget that.

"DOG AGILITY IS SUPPOSED TO be fun!" Irina shouted to me over and over when she saw me get frustrated during class.

"Pay attention!" Irina would yell as I led Nairobi in the wrong direction.

"Watch your dog!" she'd scream as Nairobi would take off after a squirrel.

I had the hardest time staying in the moment with my dogs, and frankly, Irina's yelling didn't help. Every time she'd snap at me, I would feel a burst of rebellious anger. *Be quiet! Explain it to me calmly!*

Nairobi didn't pay any attention to Irina's outbursts. All he knew was that he wasn't the one in trouble, and he was getting to run and jump and play. My thoughts were more complicated. I wanted to yell back at Irina. But of course, I didn't—although I did send her furious looks behind her back. On our bad days, I worked hard, kept my mouth shut, and raced home after class. Occasionally, though, we had amazing classes. It was disconcerting to move so fluidly from resenting Irina to completely enjoying and appreciating her. It was puzzling. Just when I thought I couldn't bear one more difficult class, everything would go perfectly: My thinking and acting were in tune. Nairobi responded in kind, and Irina would be open and encouraging. On those days, Irina and I would talk.

During class one day, Irina gave me a lecture on good handling. "If you don't give Nairobi the right direction, you frustrate him. He's naturally enthusiastic. For a dog, it's all about the experience of the moment. He shows up ready for a good experience. Bad handling or confusing signals are discouraging to him."

This hit home, not only about my lack of training skills, but also about how I was feeling around Henry since our engagement. We had a lovely peak for about six months, and then we hit the Earth with a thud. That sparkling yellow diamond brought myriad expectations into the mix, and, although the subtle messages the ring telegraphed went unspoken, new demands were forming as if on cue. Henry now wanted me to be available to him—and agree with him—all the time; he expected me to behave like a wife—or at least his idea of what a wife should be. I suddenly wanted Henry to be nice, and my impatience with his impolite or thoughtless behavior was growing. One would think I had never even met him.

Suffice it to say, we weren't handling the situation—or one another—very well.

One of my deep frustrations with Henry was his complaining; he complained all the time, every day, about everything. This was nothing new, but suddenly, every complaint seemed like a personal affront. "What a beautiful day!" I'd say. "It's going to rain," Henry would counter with a frown. *But it's not raining now! You just ruined my feeling about the beauty of the day!* I would rage inside, not once noticing the uselessness—and negativity—of my inner protests. A drive in traffic elicited a lecture from Henry about the incompetence of Los Angeles city planners; a day at work produced a diatribe about the stupidity of clients; a dinner at a nice restaurant equaled a critique of the chef's lack of talent in the kitchen.

Henry liked to kvetch. I liked to exaggerate the positive.

Henry's friends accepted him the way he was and actually relied on his appraisals. I once sat at dinner with his "foodie" friends, and the only conversation at the table was a critique of the meal—course by course.

"I like the texture of this salmon mousse, but the taste . . . I don't know," said one dining companion.

"He totally missed the sweetness . . . It's lacking. What do you think, Henry?"

"Unacceptable," another friend added, looking at Henry for confirmation.

To which Henry concluded, "The reviews were wonderful, but this food is under par. This is a total disappointment."

The disapproving atmosphere at the table left me feeling as disappointed as my dinner partners—even though I had really liked the food.

While their opinions were certainly more knowledgeable than mine, I didn't give them one ounce of credit. My inner voice was engaged in my own harsh critique—of them.

I told these stories to Irina—and more. I was on a roll.

"When we're driving, Henry complains loudly about the traffic instead of just accepting that we're crawling along. I hate it. He'd rather assault me with his negativity than spend the moment having a nice conversation with me. It makes me crazy. He destroys a perfectly good moment with his anger. He rants, yells, my heart starts pounding, I feel sick to my stomach, and I just want to run away."

"Well, of course," Irina answered, "that would make anyone miserable . . . but Henry is doing what he likes."

"What do you mean?"

"Henry likes to complain, right?"

"Right."

"So, he's doing what he likes . . . but that's different than liking what he's doing."

What did you just say?

"Doing what you like is one thing. Henry likes to complain. It serves a need for him. It's a habit, whatever. It's how most people behave. Doing what you like is selfish, though, especially if it's hurting those around you. You Americans seem to be quite invested in doing what you like. But dogs? They like what they do. And if they don't like it, they don't do it."

I noted Irina's crack about "you Americans," but I let it go. I was still trying to grasp what she was saying.

"Henry is doing what he likes. Even though it's upsetting his fiancée . . . even though it might eventually cost him his fiancée, he feels entitled to do what he likes."

IT TOOK ME A FEW days to absorb this. I began thinking about my own behavior: *Was I "doing what I liked" when I got mad at Henry?*

Oh my gosh. Yes.

And I certainly didn't like what I was doing.

And my angry rebellious thoughts about Irina? Were those also a sense of emotional entitlement?

Yes.

Not a pretty picture here.

As I watched Nairobi and Sheila wake up and go through their day throughout the following week, I saw evidence that they *like* what they do. They wake up with tales wagging. They are happy at the dawn of each day. When I prepare their food and make them sit and look at me before I release them to eat—they like it. My dogs like to work for their food. When I take them for walks and go through our routine commands—stop, sit, look at me, stand, heel—I can feel their "liking" for what they're doing. And when we simply take a walk, with no work involved, they also like it. If they didn't, they'd drag their feet and hang back—as I've seen some dogs do—instead of walking jauntily beside me.

How profoundly different from the human experience, particularly my own.

What an amazing transformation would be possible if I could commit to liking what I'm doing . . . at any given moment.

Dogs naturally come to an activity with a certain amount of enthusiasm. A dog doesn't care about waiting in the car, about a changed routine. Dogs don't bring negative emotions into a situation. If they don't like something, they simply won't do it. And when they like what they're doing . . . they are doing what they like.

For people, traffic, bad food, chores . . . are all equal if you decide to *like* what you're doing. It's possible to find something to relate to in the moment.

Traffic? Turn up the radio.

Bad food? Have another glass of wine.

Chores? Physical effort feels good . . . and burns calories.

Henry's negative opinions? They're *his*—let him have them and I'll be content with, and enjoy, my own.

So, how can this transformation happen? It's just a state of mind, but it needs to be encouraged.

Nairobi and Sheila don't like rain. I think the wet ground feels strange to them. When I take them out in the rain, they lower their heads and pick up their feet sharply as if they were walking on hot coals. But when I coax them in a positive tone of voice, give them treats, and act happy about the rain, both dogs join in on the fun. They seek to "like." It's their nature.

Why couldn't I be the same way?

I know why. I think too much. My mind is always in a whirl of to do's, questions, random thoughts, ideas about the past, present, and future—and judgments about everything.

My mind is quite spectacular at helping me squirm out of the pleasure or difficulty of a moment by conveniently hosting and serving up thoughts of what an experience *might* be like instead of what it is. My busy mind compares the present experience to a perfect idea I cooked up somewhere along the line . . . instead of being present.

I have lived through moments where my mind was running a visually detailed scene in Technicolor that was not actually happening. *Wow.* How could I possibly be "liking" anything if I'm running a movie in my head?

I'm sure I'm not alone here. The noise of a complex, demanding world, not to mention the noise in your head, can just plain interfere with living life—and the enjoyment of it.

We stop expecting pleasure. We stop looking for it. We can't even be coaxed into it.

Even sadder, we learn to delay it.

I know so many people who are unhappy with their careers and their love lives, but they remain in their stagnant job or unhappy relationship for some nebulous payoff in the future.

Dogs could care less about the future. They want to have fun right now.

I think dogs have the right idea.

JUST TRY IT

Irina approaches every aspect of teaching a dog something new with this one concept: Try it . . . you might like it.

"If a dog takes the jump, enjoys the experience, gets a good cookie on the other end, he might want to do it again. If a dog doesn't like it, he doesn't. Some dogs simply don't take to agility. But the experience of jumping or sitting when told or climbing the A-frame may prove delightful, and then there's that added bonus of the treat. Remember, when it comes to new, strange things, dogs need to be taught that the journey of the activity is all pleasurable, and we reinforce this with praise and treats."

Training Nairobi on the teeter after his unfortunate accident was a perfect example. He'd originally accepted the teeter because I'd asked him to, and he seemed to like it, but after the accident, he was wary. Taking time with him, treating him with cookies, and staying positive eventually changed the way he saw the teeter. While he never races to the teeter now, he does walk toward the obstacle confident that nego-tiating the narrow board that bangs down on the other side will bring him praise and tasty food. He's cautious, but he's enjoying himself.

Working with Nairobi on the teeter was illuminating for me because it gave me a clear picture of the value in revisiting the "site of the accident" and changing the emotions attached to it. Focusing on the pleasure of the journey instead of the ultimate destination is transformative.

This idea was profoundly important to me as a writer. The act of writing is entirely pleasurable for me. The goal of presenting or selling my work is not. Sometimes the worry about whether anyone would buy my creative efforts would paralyze me. I would sit for days just worrying. If I was in Nairobi's place, I would have sat in front of the teeter and agonized over the possibility that I might fall off and hurt myself.

Once I changed my focus to enjoying the pleasure of the journey, my entire writing life changed. I couldn't wait until the sun set so I could start working on my novel. I began looking forward to the pleasure I was going to have.

ONE AUTUMN DAY ON THE agility field it started to rain heavily. Nairobi's response to rain is to attempt to shrink himself into as tiny a ridgeback as he can manage; his tail curls under, his head lowers, he squints his eyes, his ears flatten against his head, and he literally contracts his muscles. It's as if Robi imagines that a dry space exists between the raindrops, and if he squeezes himself small enough, he just might fit there. And if this display isn't enough to communicate his misery, he shivers pathetically.

As the rain poured down on my incredible shrinking dog, my thought was to put him back in the car and head home, but Irina had other ideas.

"Come on," she called out. "Let's keep going!"

I was already soaked through to the skin, it was cold outside, and I wasn't keen on getting even more uncomfortable, but I decided to give it a try.

"Let's try a straight line of jumps," Irina suggested.

The course was laid out with a series of five jumps in a row with two tunnels, one on each end. I treated Robi with cookies at the start, but he would not sit. His rear end hovered an inch above the ground, but with a bit of encouragement and lots of treats, he finally sat down in the mud with his eyes closed, looking absolutely wretched. I called out, "Come jump!" and what happened was a perfect illustration of "try it . . . you might like it."

Robi picked up speed, flew over the five jumps, dashed through the tunnel and then wouldn't stop. Irina and I laughed hysterically as Robi ran his own course, looking for jumps to take with a wild look in his eyes. He took the jumps backwards and forwards, he went through the tunnels over and over like he was chasing a rabbit through them, and then he jumped over the tunnel instead of running through it. He seemed to like that so much, he did it again and again. He slid in the mud as he took the corners, smashing into the edge of the tunnel a couple of times, but he kept on going. Robi likes an audience and the harder Irina and I laughed, the crazier he went, the bolder he got, and Nairobi seemed to grow in front of my eyes, transforming into Robi— the crazy, rain-loving ridgeback.

Finally, exhausted, he barreled into me, jumping wildly, covering me in mud.

He tried it.

He more than liked it.

And despite my initial lack of enthusiasm for running in the cold, wet rain, I liked it, too. Growing up in a suburb of Boston, we always played outside when it was raining, and I wondered when exactly I had stopped playing in the rain? Then I realized it wasn't the rain; it was that I'd stopped playing. I was living a somber life with Henry, and I realized the only time I was purely happy in that kid-like, joyful way was when I was running with the dogs. Doubts about my choices began to creep into my mind, and when I returned home from that great, messy day and saw Henry's look of disapproval reserved for whenever I did something wild or silly, I could feel myself shrink up inside, just like a ridgeback in the rain.

IN ONE MOMENT

I'm running the course, trying to remember where the next obstacle is, and, meanwhile, Nairobi has gotten excited and decided to run his own version of the course. He's somewhere across the field having a grand time for himself. I'm so caught up in my mind, I don't even notice.

Irina shakes her head. "The sport is called '*dog agility!*'" she yells. "Don't forget about the *dog!*"

Right.

There is a point in learning agility where your mind is simply absorbed with thinking about what you're doing, but the very act of thinking takes you completely out of the moment . . . and separates you from your dog.

At the beginning of training, the hardest thing is to get the dog to stay in front of the jump while you walk past it. You practice that over and over. Stay . . . Stay . . . Stay . . . Come, jump!

Then it's hard to get a dog to take more than one jump at a time.

Then it's nearly impossible to get the dog to run ahead of you toward a sequence of jumps. The first time I tried to send Robi ahead of me with a "go, jump," he looked at me with a perplexed look. "Aren't you coming, too?" he seemed to be asking.

Finally, it's a challenge to guide the dog over a course and to teach him how to change direction.

When you first begin training in agility, the dog watches your every movement, but after awhile, after years of training, the dog doesn't watch you; he's looking for jumps to take, and he's seeing the directions you're showing him out of his peripheral vision.

And to do any of this, you have to stay in real time. You have to get out of your head.

There is a lot of technique involved in the sport and Irina is a very specific teacher. She often explains the course and walks it with me without the dogs. Sometimes she spits out the course layout very quickly from across the field, and I'm left to my own devices to figure out how to do it correctly.

"Start at the 'coyote' jump, dog on your left," she yells. "Take the blue wing, the red wing, then send your dog to the right side of the tunnel. Take the dog walk, then finish on the white and blue wing jumps."

When I hear Irina's instructions, my mind generally goes blank, but I walk the course, miming where my hands go, which is the "come" hand, which is the "go" hand, and I end up with a tentative plan of attack.

Irina watches.

I walk the course one more time and feeling more confident, I go to the car and get Nairobi. Sheila howls; she doesn't like to be excluded from the action. Robi looks rattled; he doesn't like it when Sheila gets upset.

I walk Robi to the coyote jump, take off his leash, and call, "Come, heel."

Robi moves to my left and sits. I give him a cookie.

"Stay," I call out as I walk away from him past the first jump.

Robi watches me. Sheila howls.

I run the course once more in my mind, but by the time I look back at Robi—it couldn't have been more than five seconds—Robi has broken position and is standing with a glazed look in his eyes. Sheila is still howling. I walk back to him and start again.

This time, I stop thinking and don't take my eyes off of him as I walk out past the jump.

"Stay."

Now he's watching me, getting excited. *Any moment now and I get to run!*

"Come, jump!"

And we're off. I run toward the blue jump, left arm extended, showing him the next jump, run to the red, left-right-left footwork for the front cross, right hand treat, but Robi nearly barrels into me because I'm too slow. He grabs his cookie anyway and heads for the tunnel. We're dancing crazily; it's a Carol/Nairobi mash-up, but Robi flies over the last jump and then races back to me to get his cookies. He leaps up and licks my face.

"That was okay," Irina calls out. "But you need to get into your front cross quicker. You're slowing him down."

I walk Robi back to the starting line, put him in a stay, and do it again. This time, I follow Irina's instructions and get in front of the tunnel quicker and finish my front cross elegantly just as he's starting to take the red jump. He grabs the treat from my waiting hand and scoots into the tunnel and out and races up the dog walk and takes the last two jumps, flying. It feels like we're dancing . . . beautifully.

"Good," Irina calls.

Perfect.

Real time: an hour-and-a-half of straight running and working in the present tense. Driving home, I'm as relaxed as I've ever been. There are no worries in my mind.

The dogs are conked out in the back of the car.

WHEN I AM IN THE MOMENT with my dogs during agility class, I am always surprised by what I see. Even something as simple as putting Nairobi in a "stay" and walking out in front of him reveals his state of mind. I watch his face and he may be looking at me, ready to go, or his eyes might be wandering to the left, and when I follow his gaze, I see a squirrel on the field. He might have that glazed, unfocused look, which usually means he's listening to Sheila whining or barking in the car and he's conflicted—he wants to run back to the car and give her a kiss, and he wants to run the course.

Running beside Nairobi, I can see him looking toward a jump

on the left, and I can correct him with a "right, jump" and watch as he shifts his attention and heads toward the correct jump.

In the middle of a course, I can see Nairobi's quick glance in my direction asking, "Which way now?"

If I'm paying attention, I can also tell when excitement is gripping him, and if I'm quick enough, I can stop him before he starts running wildly, taking any jump within sight.

When I stay in the moment on the agility field, I've found exhilaration and confusion. Irritation and joy. A skinned knee and a heart pounding at 160 beats per minute. Happiness, anger, embarrassment . . . and shame.

One day, early on in my training, I brought Nairobi close to Irina as she was sitting in her chair, and he jumped up on her.

"Carol!" she yelled. "Control your dog! Don't *ever* let him jump on me!"

I was shocked. Nairobi is a big dog, but he was just being friendly. He *loved* Irina.

"You have to keep your dog under *control,"* she yelled. "I can't risk getting hurt!"

My face flamed red.

Irina is a slight woman and she depends on a healthy body for her work. While she's fit and athletic, her small frame is vulnerable. Nairobi could have knocked her down, and she could have been injured. I later learned it had happened to her before with other dogs.

"No one thinks about *me*—all these years I've been teaching, and owners—like *you*—can't control their dogs. It's dangerous! What would happen to *my* dogs if I was hurt? How could I make a living? Pay my rent?"

Irina lectured me for a good ten minutes on my lack of common sense, on keeping my dog under control, on never letting him jump on anyone, on my lack of sensitivity; the list of criticisms was long. Battling both guilty feelings and the thought that she was overreacting, I stood still and listened.

"You are *thoughtless!* An accident with your dog could put me out of work for months! I compete *every* weekend, and what would happen to my dog's career if I'm hurt? Who would take care of *my* dogs?"

In those moments, I discovered quite a bit about the woman who'd been teaching me for a year. I saw a glimpse of her challenges, how she needed to protect herself so that she could compete—the true passion and joy in her life—how deeply responsible she felt for her three dogs, what was meaningful to her, and the fragility of it all. Like most lives, hers was pieced together with a few friends, responsibilities, passions, but it could all fall apart in an instant.

It was an awkward and awful ten minutes as her tirade washed over me. It could have been my last class. It almost was my last class.

There are many possible experiences when you stay in the moment, and countless ways to react to them. I was very tempted to leave, to get away from Irina as fast as I could. But another thought process took over.

Here I was, basically a dog agility dilettante, and there she was, a professional with international standing. The only reason Irina was working with me was because teaching brought her an income.

And how careless of me to let my guard down with my dog— even for one moment. Having raised children, I knew this. You never stop paying attention. The risk is too great. The fabric that makes up all of our lives is vulnerable. The least we can do for one another is to be aware of that.

I apologized, but Irina wouldn't listen or look me in the eye. But she'd exposed herself in a raw way—we were both witnesses to it. It's extraordinary how revealing anger can be. After her rant was over, Irina shut down; her face was pale. She was vulnerable. I hadn't argued with her or defended myself. To Irina, my silence meant respect—and safety. With a dismissive wave, I was sent home.

As odd as it may appear, that was the moment when Irina and I became friends. There was a subtle shift in our dynamic. She was still my teacher and I was her student, but I felt suddenly protective because I knew a bit more about what was at stake for her. Very soon after, she would learn what was at stake for me—and become equally protective.

Hard Lessons

chapter five

*Sometimes people and even dogs come into
our lives to reveal exactly where we are—
and where we've gone wrong.*

*The trick is to use the information to lead
you to a better, more productive place—
not always an easy task.*

Anyone who's ever owned more than one dog can always name the one that got under their skin. Often, this deeply loved dog has been tagged a loser by everyone except its owner. Perhaps the outcast label adds to the emotional connection. Or maybe we see a reflection of our own imperfect selves in these outlaw dogs. Rescue dog, sick dog, dumb dog, angry dog, or lost dog, they all have one thing in common: our wish to save them.

WHAT CAN I SAY ABOUT Sheila? First, I can tell you that Henry named her. He's clever with words and Sheila's grandfather was from Australia. "A girl is a 'sheila' in Australia," he said one day. The name stuck.

Sheila was one of a litter of two that were bred from a Swedish Champion sire and an American Champion dam. My breeder had great hopes for Sheila and her only brother; unfortunately, Sheila had an overbite and needed surgery to cap her teeth, which essentially left her unable to show. My breeder had too many dogs to care for and asked if I would take her. I said yes—of course.

She came to me at five months—a big, red, nervous, silly mess who shook like a leaf and licked my hands incessantly. Nairobi, who was a year and a half, was delighted with his new playmate and fascinated by her nervousness; he couldn't take his eyes off of her. Zoe, part Doberman, part German shepherd, was suspicious of the newcomer, as she was of everything and everyone. Zoe was pretty neurotic so when Sheila came into my life, I wasn't overly concerned. I had some experience.

Sheila had a thing about floors. It didn't matter what kind—marble, tile, or wood—if it wasn't carpeted she wasn't touching it.

Unfortunately, all the rooms in my house, save for the hallway, had hardwood floors. Sheila would not walk on them. Instead, she'd walk daintily along the carpeted hallway and stare into all the rooms from the safety of the doorway.

Using what I'd been taught, I began training her: first step, here's a cookie. Take another step, get a cookie. This went on and on. I even laid a trail of treats across the wood floor in the living room. Watching her attempt to get to the treats was dismaying. From her spot on the carpet, she'd stretch her neck out to get to the first few. Then, with three legs anchored on the carpet, she'd put one foot on the floor and reach a few more. Then two feet on the carpet, two on the floor. After that she'd stop. She'd lie down on the carpet and stare mournfully at the rest of the treats. After about a month, she discovered the couch and decided it was a safe zone in the middle of the hard-floor battle-field. She'd eat all the treats she could reach, then take flying leaps into the room, wolf up the remaining treats like a vacuum, and jump up on the couch where she promptly curled up in a ball. To get her off the couch, however, I needed to drag her shaking body or carry her.

Outside the safety of her bed, Sheila looked scared, as if she'd suf-fered some great trauma. Her head would lower, her eyes would shift back and forth, and she'd hide between my legs—quite a feat for a big dog.

There were many things to be afraid of around the house. The wind was a big one. The sound of the wind had Sheila shaking so hard her teeth would chatter, but when the wind blew a shade or a curtain, she would bolt between my legs or try to climb into my lap.

The sight of another dog brought out a different side of her per-sonality; it transformed her into the most aggressive animal I'd ever handled. Beginning around a year old, she'd charge at a passing dog, teeth bared, barking, pulling on the leash, lifting her front legs off the ground as if ready to pounce. Walking Nairobi and Sheila together was a huge challenge. I constantly worried that we'd run into another dog and Sheila would attack.

But Sheila had some redeeming qualities as well. She was beautiful and affectionate. Her coat was a deep, shiny red, her musculature was perfect, her legs were long and strong, her eyes were sweet, and she was a kisser. Hands, feet, face—any exposed part of my body was a reason for Sheila to come kiss me.

She was also a sympathetic, responsive dog when she was at home—and the wind wasn't blowing. She obeyed commands quickly, followed me from room to room, curling up at my feet wherever I ended up, but she was also uncomfortably subservient—almost too anxious to please.

Outside of the house, however, she was pure hound—with a strong prey instinct, a tendency to wander away, and a love of the chase. But she was also neurotic and easily scared. It was a dangerous combination.

One day I took Nairobi and Sheila out for a hike in the Santa Monica Mountains. I had Nairobi out of the car, his leash fastened, but as I opened the door to get Sheila, she bolted out of the car, ears flattened, and took off into the woods at a high speed. I'd never had a dog get loose like that and she was running fast, impervious to my calls. It was as if she was possessed by fear and her primitive instinct kicked in: *run*. When hounds are in flight, they can't see anything but their prey. In Sheila's case, she was just running and could easily have become lost in the California mountains or attacked by coyotes or even a mountain lion.

Nairobi was frantic; he knew this wasn't supposed to be happening, and as I ran after her, pulling him along, he barked loudly. That slowed her down and she started to circle back to us. I stopped running, my heart pounding from adrenaline and fear, and stood still, calling her softly. Starting with large circles, she got closer and closer until she ended up crawling on her belly toward us. I grabbed her collar, got them both back in the car, and drove home, my hands shaking.

In agility, Sheila was at her worst. From the moment we got in the car to drive to the field, she trembled. She was wary, suspicious, and frightened of Irina, of the jumps, and of the obstacles. It was a dramatic display; Sheila was fixated on resisting anything new. Irina thought that agility would help Sheila build confidence and lessen her fear-based aggression, but as time went on, even Irina was ready to concede defeat. Sheila was a stubborn dog. I'd try to call her over a jump, and Sheila would go around it. We tried the jumps lower and lower and, finally, Sheila stepped over. One of her phobias was that no one could approach her from behind. When Irina would try, Sheila would swing around violently to keep Irina in front, nearly knocking me over. After weeks of hearing stories of my near misses with dogs in my neighborhood and observing Sheila's aggressive barking at other dogs that happened to be on the field, Irina told me I should give Sheila back to the breeder.

"She's unbalanced and dangerous. Someone is going to get hurt. And Nairobi is suffering. He's a great dog and his potential will be limited. Her neuroses will dominate his life, and yours."

"But I can't give her back," I protested. "I love her."

"She's too much for you."

"I can learn. I can handle her. I just need more time."

Irina wasn't moved. "Ask your breeder to give you another dog."

"I can't."

I didn't agree with Irina's assessment. I thought she was being cruel.

I believed that love alone would save my damaged dog.

"Hah!" Irina said, shaking her head as she walked away.

OFF BALANCE

Sometimes you think everything is going along smoothly in your life until a difficulty emerges. It doesn't have to be a big, dramatic event. It can be a simple irritation or inconvenience. Your reaction to this stress, however, is always a good gauge for how stable, strong, and balanced you really are.

It turned out that the arrival of Sheila revealed that I wasn't doing all that well.

The first thing I noticed was how fearful I had become. Sheila bolting out of the car, her aggression toward other dogs, left my heart racing. But it didn't stop there. My heart seemed to be racing all the time. I imagined disasters with the dogs, just like I used to worry about bad things happening to my children when they were very young. It got so bad that even walking the dogs filled me with anxiety and dread. The thought of running into a stray dog and finding myself in the middle of a dogfight kept my heart beating wildly during our walks. I was hyper-aware of danger, very emotional, easily frustrated, and constantly worried. I wasn't entirely sure how I'd gotten there, but I was completely out of balance.

Sheila and I suddenly had a lot in common.

Then Henry and I bought a house, or rather Henry bought the house and sort of pressured me into moving in with him. It happened so fast, I didn't really connect with the implications of it all. The housing market was in a frenzy—multiple bids were happening on every house up for sale. Though we'd talked about buying a house, to me it remained a distant possibility; it wasn't supposed to happen now.

It was a rainy day. Henry called excitedly and told me he'd found our house, and before I knew it we were the owners of a lovely Spanish-styled home in Santa Monica. Henry was so enthusiastic I just gave in—and up. Even though Henry and I had been engaged for awhile, we'd never officially lived together or even date. To be honest, I never really pictured an actual marriage to Henry. I'd dragged my feet about planning a wedding. I told myself I was waiting for a long stretch of happy moments between us, but the long stretch of happiness never appeared. And now I was faced with the reality of moving in with a man with whom I wasn't all that content.

I started dating Henry well before the ridgebacks and agility training. The first time I met Henry, I believed I understood who he was: an intellectually gifted man with a dark side, a steady man who was often charming and always sarcastic. He loved puns and crossword puzzles, but couldn't put his own life together quite so neatly. Henry was always disappointed—in life, love, and family. Nothing and no one met his expectations or exacting standards. Basically, he was unhappy, and though he professed that he'd given up on being surprised and dazzled by love, it seemed to me that there was a hopeful glint in his eyes when he looked at me. That was my cue.

Why did I sign up for the assignment? I wanted to save him. I thought I could make him smile and make him believe in love, in me, and by doing that, I would be loved like no other.

It was his mind I loved first; he was the smartest man I'd ever met. Then, it was his predictability. I loved the fact that I knew what he was going to do, say, think. I, on the other hand, felt changeable, moveable, often uncertain. I was a single mother, holding my life together with a brave front that covered my deep anxiety and uncertainty. To me, Henry was like a mountain. He was the calm in a storm. He had certainty. And he cooked—beautifully. He fed me, was reliable, turned up when he said he was going to, was faithful, passionate, and asked me to marry him. I was the optimist to his pessimist. I was a believer, he was an atheist. Yes, the chemistry was good.

But actually, I was wrong about Henry, even as I held fast to that picture of him as a pillar of strength. Henry was insecure, needy, and in need of a lot more support than I ever knew. Turns out, I was actually the strong one, but it took me a long time to figure that out.

The fact was, we were a mismatch from the start. And I'm very sure we never really knew one another very well. From the first moment we met, we saw illusions. In Henry's mind, I was a vivacious, positive, capable woman. While I do have those qualities, I'd say they were my "presentation" mode. In my day-to-day life, I'm a sensitive, reflective loner. To me, Henry was powerful, clever, and passionate. In reality, he was moody, sensitive, and unsure. We fell in love with those original perceptions we had of each other. Our true selves never even said hello.

Our fights began almost immediately after dating, but they weren't exactly fights; they were an accumulation of hurt feelings that resulted in distance and silence. We would break up by not returning phone calls. That was it. After three days of an unreturned phone call or an unanswered email, we would both conclude in our minds that it was over. A month would go by. At first, I'd be angry. By the second month, I'd be weepy. By the third month, I'd be missing him so desperately I couldn't eat. Then one or the other of us would send a test email. Then a flurry of emails, pages and pages of hurt feelings, and recriminations and apologies, and then we would rush into one another's arms for another three months of bliss until the process started all over again. It was exhausting, exhilarating, and quite stupid, but we simply could not stay away from one another. We were deeply attached, but unable to make one another happy.

WHEN I FIRST BROUGHT SHEILA home from the breeder, Henry rolled his eyes but didn't say much. In Henry's mind, owning three dogs was simply excessive. He didn't quite get my love for dogs, and he definitely didn't enjoy the fact that my time with the dogs translated to time away from him. It wasn't that Henry didn't like dogs; he just expected them to have a "place" and to behave in a certain way. Henry was the alpha, and dogs were, well, *pets,* and their purpose was to provide affection and companionship—without requiring a lot of work. When I first met Henry, he had an ill-mannered, sweet-tempered golden retriever named Jesse. Jesse panted constantly, pulled on his leash during walks, chased balls obsessively, and was an affectionate, almost fawning dog. When Jesse stared into your eyes, you could melt from the sheer intensity of his devotion. Henry adored Jesse. The two of them would sit for hours, Henry watching golf on television while stroking Jesse, Jesse panting, soaking up the love and staring at Henry. They were a perfect fit.

I always thought Henry wished I was a bit more like Jesse.

Jesse was aging fast; he had lost his eyesight and for a short while when Henry travelled for work, Jesse was integrated into my household with Robi, Sheila, and Zoe, who was also elderly. The ridgebacks took to Jesse, and they shepherded the poor blind guy around, flanking him so he didn't bump into walls. It was mayhem whenever Jesse would visit, but we managed. Jesse's care required eye drops every few hours to save his one remaining eye, but he didn't seem to mind. Jesse was a good-natured, happy dog. Blind or not, he was always up for an adventure or a snack.

At the time, I lived in a two-story house with a wide wooden staircase. One morning, as the dogs clamored down the stairs for breakfast, Jesse stopped in his tracks with a panicked look on his face. I knew he was in trouble. As I rushed up the stairs to him, he collapsed on the ground and wouldn't move. The other dogs circled and sniffed. Nairobi gave Jesse a kiss. I called Henry, who came immediately. As soon as Jesse saw Henry, he struggled to stand, tail wagging. It was heartbreaking. We managed to get Jesse in the car, but I knew he was in pain. His tail kept wagging, big brown eyes staring lovingly in Henry's direction.

Jesse's spleen had ruptured, and by the time Henry got him to the vet, there wasn't much that could be done. Henry never talked about his grief. I don't even know if he cremated Jesse and kept the ashes. If I mentioned how much I missed Jesse, and what a wonderful dog he was, Henry wouldn't respond. Even though I knew Henry missed Jesse terribly, he kept his pain to himself. That was the one trait that Henry and I shared—deeply painful events were experienced in private, alone.

Henry tried to warm up to my dogs, but ridgebacks are not golden retrievers. Their personalities are simply different. Where retrievers are naturally affectionate, gregarious, and adoring, ridgebacks are more somber and intense and selective about their affection and to whom they give it. For a dog lover who is seeking a compliant, eager-to-please dog, a ridgeback would pose a challenge. My dogs respected Henry, but were wary and distant with him while being playful and affectionate with me. This was simply their nature. Their allegiance is singular, quite specific. And their response to Henry was also based on their experience of my relationship with Henry, which had been off and on. Ridgebacks read their owner's loyalties and react accordingly. They are quite discriminating and sensitive to the vagaries of human alliances.

Henry felt left out. Without Jesse by his side, he didn't have a dog ally. He did try to create a relationship with the ridgebacks, but this trio didn't have any chemistry. While I enjoyed the fact that Nairobi and Sheila disappeared to their beds when I was working, Henry wanted them alert, by his side, watching golf. They would have none of it. It was frustrating, and sad, to watch.

NO MEANS NO . . . SORT OF

"I broke up with Henry," I said to Irina.

"Really?"

"Yes. I mean I think I did."

"What happened?" she asked . . .

WHEN I THINK ABOUT HOW many times I made this statement to Irina, it's shocking. And each time Henry and I would get back together, Irina would say, "That's good. Let's see how it goes this time."

Thinking back, I can never remember exactly why we broke up, what the incidents were, but I remember how I felt. I had that uncomfortable, hollow feeling inside that I was in the wrong place with the wrong person. The fights, whatever they were about, overshadowed the "us"; but really, there was no "us." It was him and me, circling around each other, trying to fit in, trying to be important to one another.

It must have been hard for Irina to watch me suffer. She doesn't believe in voluntary suffering. She thinks we should all be more like dogs, seeking pleasure and happiness whenever we can. I must have seemed like a strange anomaly to her—a woman hell-bent on seeking heartbreak and reliving it over and over again.

"Invite Henry to class so he can watch you and Nairobi," Irina said one day.

"He won't come," I said.

"Sure he will," Irina said. "I'll be charming and he can see how well you're doing with Nairobi. Invite him. I want to meet him."

Henry came once. Irina was at her talkative best. I watched as she tried to get Henry interested, and she even made him laugh a few times.

He was pleasant to Irina and took a few pictures. He never commented on his visit except to tell me one day that I shouldn't go to agility so much. It took up too much of my time.

Henry and I did have some great times together. We did best when we were alone; socializing with others was always difficult for us. He didn't like my friends, especially my male friends, and he didn't really have any friends, only business acquaintances, work relationships, and a few superficial friendships based on his two passions: food and golf. I think I was Henry's only real friend. Our best times were when we travelled to Europe every summer, though we did fight on several vacations and spent gloomy days not talking. Each time I would go back to Henry after one of our separations, I was determined; I vowed to accept him for who he was, abandon expectations of more loving behavior, and try to fit in to what he needed from a partner. But underneath my determination was fear;

I was afraid to lose him, to admit that I couldn't handle his complexity or make him happy. I was afraid to face the possibility that we were destined to fail.

It wasn't just Henry, though. Fear had become my companion; it was the underlying condition in my life. Perhaps it was due to the many years I'd spent fending for myself and my children alone, but anxiety and fear had become mainstays. I had purposefully chosen a difficult man and two difficult dogs, but instead of relaxing with my choices, I was gripping the leash tightly, afraid to find out what would happen if I simply let go.

So, when Henry bought the house, I planned to move in. In preparation, I went through boxes and boxes of old files. I shredded papers, tossed things away, picked through kid memorabilia, old toys, photos, and threw away remnants of the past twenty years of my life. I looked through my childhood report cards, my wedding pictures, my divorce papers—each single item seemed like a witness to failure or loss. I'd begun each one of those phases in my life with such hope, but the result of all of that happy anticipation had brought me here. And where was that exactly? A place that wasn't secure; I was in a merry-go-round of a relationship that wouldn't slow down long enough for me to hop on and take a proper seat. I was scared. And sad. I began to cry—and couldn't stop. I knew I was feeling sorry for myself, but my rational mind wouldn't kick in to snap me out of my emotional fog. I just couldn't connect all the things I'd been through—raising my kids on my own and building a career from scratch—with the life

I was moving to. My life with Henry. There was no joy in me. I felt like I was facing a life sentence in prison.

If my personal crisis wasn't enough, my oldest dog, Zoe, was falling apart. She was deaf, half-blind, incontinent, covered in tumors, and riddled with arthritis and advanced hip dysplasia. At fourteen, sick as she was, Zoe was still hell on wheels, and she was aggressive with everyone, including the ridgebacks. She bit them viciously when they came near. I knew she was close to death, but she was so dear to me. I was simply weak, even selfish. I loved her. I didn't want to let her go. And I also didn't want to face another loss. I coaxed her with tempting food when she wouldn't eat, stroked her for hours at a time, and willed her to stay with me.

One day, Henry suddenly announced that Zoe could not move into the new house with us. I would like to report that I stuck up for Zoe and told Henry to go to hell . . . but I didn't. I actually froze up inside. I was shocked by his words. And they had absolutely nothing to do with what I was experiencing. I was in over my head with Zoe, but I didn't have the strength to face it. It was clear Zoe was in constant pain and dying, but knowing her as I did, she was game for tormenting us all until she took her last breath. It could have been a few days or a week before she would die naturally.

I've put down sick animals before. It's terrible. I've done it when the suffering was just too much, and I always trusted my connection with the animal to reveal the right moment, the moment when they communicate clearly that their time is up. It's an unmistakable look. When you see it, there is absolutely no chance of misunderstanding.

I never had that moment with Zoe. She couldn't stand up for three days and stopped eating. She'd tilt her head oddly when I sat by her, moaning softly. Her anguish was just too much to bear, and I made the decision for her. I held her in my arms as the vet gave her the injection, and Zoe looked into my eyes. Imagined or not, I saw recrimination.

Partly, the accusing look was Zoe's character. She was a tough old bitch, a fighter. I loved that about her. But what floated anchorless in my mind was Henry's proclamation that Zoe couldn't come to the new house. His words were shameful—but I couldn't get them out of my head. Did I end her life prematurely? Or did I do the responsible, caring thing for my suffering dog? I believe that I made a compassionate, responsible decision—I know this much about myself—but Henry's proclamation overshadowed my certainty. He tried to take ownership of something that was inherently mine. My relationship with Zoe and my assessment of her suffering should have been the only factors to consider. Henry's words colored the situation, and they interfered in a deeply subversive way; the words left room for self-doubt. I never forgave Henry for that. I've also never forgiven myself for leaving room in my heart for those questions and for not fully honoring my steward-ship. And sadly, I will always live with the reality of the fact that I was with a man who could even utter those words.

But truly, Zoe's accusing look was far more personal and to the point: *What the hell is wrong with you? Snap out of it! Stop crying! Push back! Stand up for yourself!*

She was a scrappy, very wise dog.

An animal's life is a responsibility that I take very seriously, and while I don't believe in sentimentality when it comes to a suffering animal, I do believe that a clear, conscious, rational, compassionate state of mind is needed when making the decision to terminate an animal's life. To me, it is required by every spiritual and moral law in this universe.

Zoe's death haunted me.

I left my home, two dogs in tow, and I moved in with Henry.

I was a total wreck.

Day-to-day life with Henry was difficult. Suddenly, rules appeared: I couldn't choose a couch, the color of the paint, or the arrangement of the furniture. We had to use *this* set of sheets, not *those*. It had to be *this* chair, not *that* one. One morning, I awoke in our bedroom and still half asleep, I had the distinct impression that I was in a hotel suite—a gorgeous, exotic room in a faraway place. I lazily wondered where I was and waited for consciousness to signal my whereabouts. Then I realized with a small panic that this was my room, in my home.

I tried to insert myself into the decision-making, but I was rebuffed, ignored, overruled at every turn.

"I'd like to put my couch in the living room."

"No. I have the perfect couch in storage," Henry said. "It was my father's. It's Spanish-styled and will fit fine. You should give yours away or sell it."

"All the furniture doesn't have to be Spanish, Henry," I countered. "We can mix and match styles."

"I don't think so."

"But that couch is huge. I don't like it and it's too big for the room. Maybe we could buy a smaller one? That we both like."

"No. It will be fine."

I walked out of room and into the backyard, so frustrated I couldn't speak.

"The yard is large, maybe later on we can put in a spa?"

"No. I don't like pools or spas. I've had so many houses with pools, but I never use them."

"I do."

Henry didn't answer.

"I think my painting will look nice over the fireplace," I ventured.

"No. Mine will look better."

Oh my God.

THERE WAS A BATTLE GOING on and Henry was hell-bent on gaining territory. I was losing, room by room. I finally received a hard-won concession; I got to choose the drapes for the window near my office.

I felt so conflicted about those drapes, though. They took a month to arrive, and even though they were beautiful, they didn't fit in with the rest of the house. They were subtle, feminine, elaborate in volume, but still quite delicate. I loved the way the light hit the silk fabric and revealed the subtle blue/green hues. I found my eyes constantly straying to them. I loved them. They were the representation of me. But they were drapes.

The rest of the house took shape around me; it was heavy, dark, and masculine. The ridgebacks followed me everywhere, tails curled under their rumps. From my office, I had a window that looked onto the street, and out of the corner of my eye, I glimpsed my drapes.

Every time I tried to express my unhappiness to Henry, I'd dissolve into tears or get infuriated—two emotional states that drove him crazy.

Since I couldn't seem to communicate rationally, I fell into a tense, numb silence. "Our" life happened around me, despite me. I was asked for my opinion after decisions were made, and I critically observed my retreat into a weak, silent, nervous woman.

I was an interloper in this house and in this life that I had carelessly backed into.

I tried hard to pull myself together and examined myself carefully to see if there was more to do to help get myself in balance. Just as I was teaching Sheila to become a more stable dog through training, I did the same with myself. I started my own training. For me, this involved rediscovering the basic elements required to keep me energized, positive, and fulfilled—and getting rid of the rest. I changed my diet to a more healthful one. I increased my fitness routine and added strength training. I went back to the spiritual reading that I had dropped somewhere along the way. I began working with an acupuncturist who touched my spiritual nature through the meditations she gave me. I invited new people into my life. My son graduated from high school, and we began preparations for college. I prayed more. I trained the dogs even more seriously. I set a deadline to finish a draft of my novel.

The most radical change I made in my life, however, was that I left Henry.

I didn't just leave. Like Sheila, I *ran*. I didn't even last three months in the new house with Henry. I was miserable from the first morning I woke up with him in our bed until the last day I woke up in the spare bedroom. I couldn't have gotten out of that situation fast enough.

High-tailing away from something difficult is nothing to be proud of. It was exactly what I was trying to teach Sheila not to do, but there I was acting exactly the same. Running away is rude, inexcusable, sometimes even dangerous, but it's a primal response from the depths of one's being. I knew I'd have to revisit my relationship with Henry at some point in the future, but at that moment, removing myself from the complexity of my problems with him was about all I could manage.

Henry wouldn't speak to me after I told him I was leaving. He was furious, deeply insulted. I packed my bags, left the house keys on the kitchen counter, a friend picked me up, and I left with the dogs. I had given all my furniture away so I moved into a house that had a recently purchased bed, an old television set, and one chair I'd saved from the fire sale of my past life. And of course, the dog beds. I sat in my chair in the middle of the empty living room, ridgebacks curled up beside me, and I breathed.

I'M NOT SURE IF SHEILA triggered my mini life crisis or if I triggered hers. And I don't know if Zoe's death was the metaphorical nail in the coffin of my relationship with Henry. The truth could probably be found somewhere in the middle.

Sometimes, people or animals come into your life and end up teaching you things you need to know or exposing vulnerabilities you didn't know you had.

I looked at Sheila now with a slightly different attitude. She was a manifestation of my undeveloped, fearful, unbalanced self. Unfortunately, Sheila was my soul mate.

It was time for both of us to grow up.

"Buck up, baby girl," I'd say to her. "We'll figure this out."

"I left Henry," I said to Irina.

For the first time, Irina said, "Good for you."

A Learning Curve

chapter six

*In agility, there is always one obstacle that
seems insurmountable. Until you face the challenge it
poses, it will bring your training to a grinding halt.*

Life is the same—only the stakes are higher.

Training Sheila was an arduous task. What would have taken
Nairobi a month to master would take Sheila a year. She made
Irina and I work every single step of the way.

*The dog walk: Irina is on one side of Sheila, I'm on the
other. Sheila is shaking and leaning on me at such a steep angle
that if I step away from her, she will fall off. Irina moves one of
her legs forward. I try to give Sheila a cookie but her mouth is
locked shut. She's too scared, too stubborn to eat. Irina moves
one of Sheila's back legs, and Sheila lies down. She won't stand
up. She won't move forward. Her tail wags.*

"This is good," Irina says. "Let her lie down and get used to this."

Irina and I chat for a moment then start again. Nudge one leg, nudge the other leg; tug her forward with the collar lightly, and encourage her.

Robi watches from the sidelines with an anxious expression on his face.

That first time on the dog walk, we spent an hour getting her across.

"She's getting better at this, building confidence," Irina said.

Really?

But Irina was right. During each class, Sheila made a small breakthrough. Resistant as she was, Sheila kept at it. Much of her motivation had to due with the fact that she loved the attention. If I left her in the car, she would yelp in protest: *"What about me?!"*

AFTER A FEW MONTHS, SHEILA SHOWED some progress, but it was inconsistent. Taking a jump, she might then wander off with a nervous, self-conscious, spaced-out look on her face. The only obstacle where she maintained concentration was the weave poles. Head down, she'd maneuver slowly but accurately through the poles. I think she felt comfortable because the obstacle required moving in a narrow space. It felt more secure to her.

Irina taught me to indulge her . . . to encourage her. Anything Sheila looked mildly interested in, we'd let her do it. She loved the tunnel. One day, we spent the entire class going in and out of the tunnel. She actually looked happy in a reserved sort of way.

She was frustrating to work with, though, and was a constant test of my patience. I was making good progress with Nairobi and then when it was Sheila's turn, I'd have to go back to the most basic level of training. I hated it. I wanted a quick solution. I wanted Sheila to be a solid, happy member of the pack.

Sheila always brought me back to Earth with a thud.

She brought me back to reality.

When I'd left Henry, I expected to hit the ground running and soar onto greatness. I wanted my life to go smoothly, easily; I wanted to be carefree, in love, writing brilliant books, and living in the south of France. Instead, I was inching along.

Sometimes progress is slow.

Some goals take a very long time to reach.

But anything you set your mind to can be accomplished. You simply have to take it one step at a time.

After six months of training, Sheila surprised both Irina and me by simply walking across the dog walk. The second time she did it, she trotted, tail wagging. Irina and I shared a look.

"Do you believe it?" I asked, incredulous.

Irina smiled. *Of course I believe it*, she seemed to say. *I'm her trainer.*

"I can't *believe* this!" I yelled.

"Don't scare her," Irina cautioned.

"*Sheila!* You are the best girl ever!"

Sheila wagged her tail and ate another cookie.

Our hard work was paying off.

We'd settled into our routine and the constant training was helping Sheila improve her overall behavior and confidence. Though she still walked close to the wall at home, she would now walk on hard floors. She listened more attentively and enjoyed working for her treats. She was better on our walks and even seemed to be developing a sense of humor. She'd whack Nairobi on his head with her paw to initiate a playful romp with him, and sometimes I'd find her on my bed when she wasn't supposed to be there, and her tail would be thumping happily. *You got me!*

I was making some progress, too. I was writing every day and running my business, but like Sheila, I had small flashes of fun and delight in between long steady bouts of shaky confidence. When my confidence was at its lowest, I missed Henry. Even his bad moods and judgmental pronouncements seemed preferable to the dead silence of my life. The only thing I had to fight with was the negative voices swirling around in my head. I wanted a sparring partner.

And life provided one.

Sheila woke up one morning, struggling to move. Her joints were swollen, her face filled with suffering, hives covered her entire body. Panicked, I raced her to the local vet, but he was out of his depth and I ended up in a critical care emergency hospital. Thousands of dollars later—after joint biopsies, blood tests, scans, and x-rays—Sheila was diagnosed with immune-mediated polyarthritis. Basically, lupus. The prognosis wasn't good. The vet started her on high doses of prednisone to throw her into remission and to control the symptoms, which included extreme joint stiffness and pain.

"We'll try the steroids and they'll make her more comfortable, but she'll gradually lose interest in activity. The pain will slow her down," the doctor said.

"Can I keep up with agility?" I asked hopefully. Agility had become the key to a happier Sheila, and I didn't want to take this away from her.

"As long as she shows an interest in it, sure," he said. "But I can't say how long that will last. I've seen dogs go through this, and they slowly lose enthusiasm for life. They just wind down."

I had a hollow feeling inside. I stroked Sheila's ears and went into my matter-of-fact crisis mode, which for me is all about facing the truth—no matter how frightening.

"How long will she live?"

The vet wore a pained expression as he answered me, "We can try immunosuppressive drugs, but without that kind of treatment, the usual course of this disease is about a year."

"Really? Are you sure?"

"There are no absolutes," he said. "She could go into remission."

I was stunned, heartbroken. I loved my crazy, beautiful dog. She was too young to be going through this. I would lie on the bed next to her, and she'd look at me with such a trusting look. It seemed impossible that I could lose her.

Not only had I fallen in love with Sheila, but Nairobi was also smitten. She was his cousin, but Nairobi treated her like his wife. Every move she made, his eyes were on her. When I walked them together, he would press his body against hers and often lean in to lick her face. The joy on his face when he kissed her or roughhoused with her was indescribable. He adored her.

With the prednisone in her system, Sheila bounced back quickly. In fact, she exhibited a whole new positive personality. But there was a trade-off. The drug, the doctor informed me, would be harmful to her system in the long run—resulting in muscular weakness and atrophy, and possible damage to the liver, pancreas, stomach, and adrenal glands. He gave me the option to switch her to another medication—one used for transplant patients to keep the immune system from attacking the new organ—but that drug had its complications as well.

The second phase of my matter-of-fact crisis mode kicked in, which is an absolute belief in miracles. I did not accept the negative prognosis for her.

I DID RESEARCH, I EMAILED everyone I knew in the dog world, I listened to owners whose own dogs had survived the disease, and I faxed her lab reports to anyone who offered to help.

I don't remember how I found holistic vet Dr. Marc Bittan, but from the first moment I spoke to him, I felt that Sheila might have a chance. He was kind, straightforward, and he explained everything in great detail. His goal was to get Sheila's disease into remission and to get her off of steroids. I didn't believe or disbelieve in any of his treatments. They simply sounded more hopeful than a short life on damaging pharmaceuticals. Dr. Bittan thought we could arrest Sheila's condition, and that there was a possibility that she could lead a normal life. He never promised me anything, but he was the one person who'd said those words. That was enough.

He began with isotherapy, which is a homeopathic remedy prepared from the patient's blood. It's given orally two to three times a day. Dr. Bittan also prescribed additional homeopathic medications and Chinese herbs. With his encouragement, I changed Sheila's diet to natural meat and vegetables in case the autoimmune disease was triggered by a food allergy to an ingredient in the commercial dog food she had been eating. We added vitamins, supplements—everything we could think of. My breeder even chimed in with some food supplement suggestions. When Sheila's belly turned black and broke out in itchy sores, I did some online research and read an article about melatonin. While melatonin is used as a sleep aid for people, there were some anecdotal references to its use for skin allergies in dogs. I mentioned it to Dr. Bittan and he encouraged me to try it. I added the melatonin to her regimen, and within a few weeks, her belly was clear and pink. It was a daily struggle, but I didn't treat her as an invalid. We kept walking, we kept training, and we kept on with agility.

WHILE IRINA STOOD FIRMLY ON the side of reason and practicality when it came to Sheila, this new turn of events changed the game; we were now dealing with a very sick dog. Irina immediately jumped into the battle to save Sheila's life. I was surprised by her support and deeply moved. I had never seen this side of her.

The steroids would work havoc on Sheila's muscles and joints, and exercise was the only way to minimize the damage by keeping them toned and strong. Not only did we continue training, I noticed that Irina challenged Sheila more. The jumps were lowered to protect her weakened joints, but Irina gave Sheila longer sequences. She also let Sheila take off after a squirrel occasionally. "Let her have some fun," Irina said. "It's good for her."

And almost miraculously, Sheila did begin to have fun. I'm not sure if it was the prednisone that helped build her confidence (Irina said steroids were like cocaine for dogs), or the work, or the fact that she was finally growing up, but Sheila became passionate about agility. On Mondays, she'd wait at the front door hours before it was time to leave. She'd jump into the car with enthusiasm, and off we'd go. At the field, she wanted to go first and howled in distress if I ran Nairobi before her. She would watch Nairobi do his runs and when it was her turn, she'd run the course as if she'd memorized it. *I know! I go to this jump next!* She ran the dog walk, she took her jumps, she weaved carefully through the poles, and she even flirted with Irina, kissing her hand and letting Irina pet her.

It was an unexpected development.

It was inspiring.

We still didn't know how Sheila would do in the long run, and we had to wean her off the prednisone without triggering her immune system, but watching her growing confidence was enough for the moment.

It was a fragile truce for me, but Nairobi was deliriously happy. He had his playmate back, and he was finally getting better food. He'd watch me closely as I cooked the meat and vegetables that both dogs now ate for dinner, probably wondering, *What took you so long?*

THE PARALLELS BETWEEN SHEILA'S dilemma and my own weren't lost on me; our paths seemed entwined. She had an autoimmune disease, which is basically the body attacking itself, and I had spent a good five years of my life putting my own emotional life in jeopardy by exposing myself to a relationship that was essentially anathema to me.

I didn't pay much attention to the symbolic resonance in our struggles because every ounce of my emotional energy went to taking care of Sheila. I had to summon all my courage to drag her from doctor to doctor, to stay calm and not baby her, to be brave in the face of her possible early death, and to move confidently through my personal and professional life.

It wasn't easy.

I spent lots of time alone. I wrote feverishly while listening to The Dave Matthews Band blaring loudly throughout my house.

The battle for Sheila's life took place over a year. It was a hot summer, a cold rainy winter, and a beautiful spring. I finished the novel. It wasn't perfect, but it was done.

During that time, I didn't date anyone. I also didn't communicate with Henry except for a few housekeeping emails—and then I did.

Blame it on Valentine's Day.

Late one morning, I was driving through Santa Monica near where I'd lived with Henry. There was a light rain, and though I was aware that I was in my old stomping grounds, my mind was on the errands I needed to run. Suddenly I spotted Henry, walking in his determined way: his head down, arms swinging, breathing heavily. My heart leapt. It was a sign.

Was it?

February 14 and there I was, staring at my ex-fiancé through a rain-spattered car window.

What were the chances? *Surely*, it was a sign.

Or a scene from a really bad movie.

My stomach flipped. My pulse raced. My mind went blank. My memory? Not readily available.

At all awkward encounters, I have a knee-jerk response: Be assertive and act.

I pulled to the curb, lowered the passenger-side window, and waited until Henry noticed me. When he did, he stopped suddenly in his tracks, sort of jumped, actually. He looked scared. Impulsively, maybe to put him at ease, I smiled broadly. Henry looked in at me warily.

"Hey," I said. "Happy Valentine's Day!"

I know this was an odd first comment after not seeing him for a year. It just came to me.

I must have been under a spell; romance plus idiocy plus amnesia plus a solid year of writing a first novel—add atmospheric rain and a dog that had nearly died—and it all adds up to really bad judgment.

"Oh, hello," Henry said.

I could hear the stress in his voice.

"Happy Valentine's Day," he said without emotion. "How is everything?"

"Good," I said, quite cognizant that it wasn't. "Everything is okay."

"How's the novel coming?"

"Almost done."

It was a surreal few moments. It was a Henry/Carol mash-up near the scene of the crime, which for us translated to a high stakes emotional poker game, cards held close to the vest. We were very, *very* calm. But the more suspicious he acted—a tilted chin, an upper body movement away from me—the more I was drawn to allay his fears.

"Good."

"It's Valentine's Day," I repeated.

"So you said."

"Don't you think that's odd . . . running into each other . . . on Valentine's Day?"

"Sure," Henry said.

"Not that we had any great Valentine's Days," I babbled, " . . . but *still*. Everything okay with you?"

Henry did grimace at my mention of our past Valentine's Days, which had all been awful. But, he rallied.

"Work is slow. My health is okay. Fine."

"Well, good seeing you."

"Yup."

And he walked away.

I drove on and knew that I was going to do something really dumb. This knowledge left me light-headed, drunk on my inevitable idiocy. I'd spent a year alone with no one around but the dogs. The strain of taking care of Sheila had worn me down. Writing a novel is hard, lonely work.

What was I thinking?

I wasn't.

Five days later, I finished the novel and sent him an email. It was long, friendly, and slightly apologetic. I felt quite loving and forgiving when I wrote it and hit the send button. Henry's response came fast and furious; it was a long and angry and accusing email. Why had I left him? I'd been cruel and stubborn and hurtful. As soon as I read his words I felt guilty. I flipped so fast into submission it was embarrassing. I was like a puppy coming face-to-face with a big, mean dog. It was as if I'd forgotten my entire experience with him. I scraped together a revisionist history in my mind; I must have been wrong all along. Our failure was mine—alone.

I did not remember or honor my experience. Suddenly, I was back in the first day of agility class with no knowledge, no idea what to do. And that familiar fear and dread was back. Why did being near Henry make me feel that way? And more to the point, why did uncomfortable feelings about someone make me want to move toward that person rather than away from them?

It was mysterious, at least to me. For a year, I'd forged ahead.

I battled insecurity, worried about Sheila, and I'd finished a novel—all while running a company by myself. I'd accomplished a lot, but it didn't protect me from the echo of the past.

I had much more to learn. My journey was really just beginning. I'd confronted certain obstacles in my personal life, but I hadn't yet reached mastery—I wasn't even close. I hadn't learned to accept my fears and move beyond them, or even with them. There were many challenges still to face and more obstacles to navigate before I could truly become the woman I wanted to be.

I was still a student.

Irina was still my teacher.

When she yelled at me, I cringed inside.

Obstacles

chapter seven

On the agility field,
dogs have handlers to help them navigate obstacles.

In life, we're on our own.

I t was mayhem on the agility field.

As Sheila became stronger, she got more confident—and she started making executive decisions. One of which was settling on squirrel-chasing as her métier.

While we had let Sheila pursue an occasional squirrel when she was ill, it was time to refocus our attention on agility. Sheila had other ideas. Class would be going along fine, and suddenly Sheila would bolt into the distance. Sometimes my back would be turned, but I could sense that she was no longer with me. Other times, she would be sitting calmly, waiting to start, and in the blink of an eye, she'd thunder after a squirrel that had dared to descend from a tree. The field where we practiced was shielded from the highway by a few buildings, but if Sheila ran past them, she could possibly end up on a busy thoroughfare.

The idea of Sheila blazing into traffic and getting hit by a car panicked me.

The reality of not being in control frightened me.

At a certain point, Sheila began to see the whole thing as a joke. It was as if she suddenly realized that she was a very big dog and there wasn't much anyone could do to stop her.

She loved it.

"Sheila!" I screamed as she powered into the distance. Despite my fear for her safety, my heart filled with emotion as I saw how strong and beautiful she looked as she ran.

Eventually, Sheila abandoned the squirrel to its scolding high up in the tree, and trotted back to me.

"Stop screaming," Irina said patiently. "Just call her once, and if she doesn't respond, stand still and wait until she disengages focus on the squirrel, and call her back to you. Once you have her by the collar, don't say a word to her and just put her in the car."

"But what if she runs into the street?" I asked anxiously.

Irina shook her head at me. "Squirrels go *up*."

Good point.

ONE DAY, SHEILA CHASED A PARTICULARLY irritating squirrel every single time I took her onto the field. I was so exhausted from the tension of that class I was nearly in tears. Sheila spent most of the class in the car, quite happy.

I stopped screaming. But I was screaming inside. It's a frustrating feeling when you realize that you can't call your dog out of danger. The squirrel nonsense showed me quite clearly that when Sheila is in her "seek prey" mode, there isn't anything I can do.

One day in class, however, Irina stepped in to help. Sheila was off-leash with me on the course, and Irina must have seen Sheila's ears perk forward and her eyes fix on a squirrel in the distance. Irina happened to be near a tree in Sheila's path, and she quickly ducked behind it. As Sheila took off, Irina jumped out from behind the tree with her arms raised over her head and yelled, "Hey! Sheila!"

Sheila stopped in her tracks, tail curled under, head lowered, and ran back to my side. I laughed. Nothing like getting scared senseless to break the squirrel spell, but I couldn't count on Irina to jump out from behind trees the rest of my life. I had to figure this out for myself.

SQUIRRELS ARE AGITATORS. THEY CHATTER, swish their tails, and provoke, especially when perched safely in a tree. They can be aggressive, fearless, and they are slow to back down. They can rivet a dog's attention so intensely the dog can't see or hear anything but that squirrel.

I get an email from Henry—my squirrel. My heart pounds. I feel excited and slightly sick at the same time.

A few months had passed since that fateful Valentine's Day, and we'd reconnected and disconnected via email several times. The content of Henry's occasional email missives were irrelevant—they all made me anxious. It could be an angry tirade, a reminder of some past slight he felt, or a question about our handyman's phone number. One time, I was too slow in responding to one of his requests, and he simply sent an email with a question mark. Like Sheila, I pounced on those emails. I was locked in hyper-focus mode with my bassett hound/squirrel.

I was riveted.

Spellbound.

Quite decisively, lost.

Henry was a fan of architectural homes. He liked to buy them, fix them up, and resell them. I was never quite sure if he was doing it for the money or to satisfy his desire to create something perfect, but either way, he was quite good at it. I wasn't surprised, then, to learn that Henry had sold the house we had lived in together. I *was* surprised to discover that he had purchased and was renovating a home less than a mile from me. I was flattered. I was scared. And I knew what was coming. In his roundabout, pride-saving "buying and selling homes" way, Henry was coming to get me. He wanted me back.

While Henry's new home was under construction, he rented an apartment in my neighborhood. The net was closing in. I fell into a dreamlike trance, waiting like an adolescent princess for my kiss. It happened one day, mid-morning, when Henry sent a provocative, sexy email. The "*principessa*" was referenced. It was exactly the right note to hit. Henry was direct, forceful, and enticing—not his usual style. The exchange snapped me out of my haze and propelled me into a keyed-up excitement. Within a day, I was knocking at his front door.

I was like Sheila, running hard and fast toward a busy street with no sense at all.

That first meeting after our separation was magical. We went straight back to the funny, happy vibe we had whenever we were in Europe. But then we talked. I was stronger than before. I'd found my voice. I stood up for myself. I wasn't fabulous or brilliant, but I was a whole lot better. Probably because of that, our reunion deteriorated quickly.

"It wasn't even that good this time," Henry wrote tersely in an email.

Oh, dear. Was he talking about the sex?

We survived that first collision, and tentatively tried to date one another. I didn't imagine it was going to end well. I actually didn't imagine much at all. I simply wasn't done. It was a mind thing—not an instinct thing.

I was so aware that being with Henry fell squarely into the bizarre category, I didn't tell anyone in my life, and I did not mention it to Irina.

SHEILA CONTINUED TO CHASE squirrels and I chased Henry. It was a whirlwind to nowhere, but exhilarating, this run—misguided, unsure of my ultimate goal, wind rushing past, and the surge of adrenaline.

What I began to realize, though, was that like Sheila, I was chasing something that was moving away from me. I was filling up the vacuum between myself and my desire because the empty space between them was uncomfortable. Like Sheila, I did not actually want to catch my squirrel; I was attached to the chase. Moving toward the object was an action that *felt* like control, but it wasn't. Sheila might have thought she was in control, but she wasn't. The squirrel was in charge. The object of my desire was moving me; I wasn't moving it. But like Sheila, I couldn't stop myself.

SCARED STRAIGHT

With all the squirrel madness, my anxiety level was high. And just in case I hadn't considered all the terrifying possibilities, Irina decided to pump up the volume.

It started with dog collars. I have always used choke collars because every obedience trainer I'd ever worked with used them. I'd never really given them much thought until Irina challenged me.

I was standing at the back of my SUV, and Irina was next to me. Both dogs had their choke collars on.

"How would you feel if I choked you when you didn't listen to me?" Irina asked provocatively.

"I wouldn't like it," I answered, puzzled by her strange question.

"Then why are you choking your dogs?"

"What do you mean?"

"You have your dogs in choke collars," Irina spat angrily.

I fell silent, thinking back to every dog obedience class I'd attended, every dog I'd owned, and every dog training show I'd seen on television. I didn't ever remember hearing that choke collars were cruel.

Are they?

Irina continued. "A choke collar mimics what dogs do to one another. It puts pressure against the neck, but there is no safety catch in a choke collar. You are threatening to strangle your dog every time you pull that chain."

Shit.

"And if you leave the collar on, it could catch on something and your dog could die."

It was useless to argue with Irina when she was on a rant. I thought choke collars were acceptable, but to her, choke collars were abusive. Martingale collars were kinder, she said. They were made of soft nylon, and while they applied pressure to the neck, they couldn't close all the way or harm the dog. I quickly went in search of the new collars.

The next issue was car transport. Most of the other agility students were competing and all of them had their dogs in kennels inside vans and SUVs. I transported my dogs loose in the car. Sheila had developed a habit of barking aggressively when she spotted other dogs from her safe perch in the back seat.

Irina lectured me on how unsafe it was to have the dogs unrestrained in the car. "Sheila's barking could cause an accident, and when a couple of hundred pounds of dog flies at your head, you'll be dead," she pronounced.

Irina was right. One time, Sheila startled me so much I actually did swerve, barely avoiding an accident.

But really, I think Irina was more concerned about the dogs.

"They could be killed in a crash or they could get loose after an accident and get hit by a car on the freeway while you're unconscious or trapped in the car!"

Nothing like sowing a little terror to drive your point home.

With disaster scenarios running through my mind, I went in search of dog kennels and put them in the car. The dogs now rode inside metal cages.

"You need to tie down the kennels," Irina said, exasperated. "You don't want them falling over if you're in a crash."

I bought bungee cords and fastened the kennels tightly.

One day, I made the mistake of telling Irina that I'd gotten tangled in the dogs' leashes and fell. We were walking close to a neighbor's fence and two dogs rushed the fence, barking. My dogs charged back and tripped me. When I fell, the dogs were shocked and rushed to my side. I had a skinned knee and felt foolish, but I was fine.

"Only use short leashes. You have to get control of your dogs."

I went out and bought one-foot leashes.

"You have no common sense," Irina pronounced. "If you have big dogs, you need to minimize the chances of them getting hurt or hurting you."

Irina's list of my infractions went on:

Bring water for your dogs when you're on long walks.

Keep their nails short; long nails can affect their muscles poorly.

Brush their teeth daily.

Don't let your dogs sniff the ground. There is no reason for them to sniff, and they could pick up a disease.

Don't let your dogs sniff one another. It's a bad habit.

Stop Robi from jumping!

Oh brother.

Irina had mentioned many of these things over the years, but she'd clearly had enough of my dilly dallying. Irina loves dogs and is slightly less sympathetic toward anyone who might harm or confuse a dog through ineptness or ignorance. Her main goal was to help dogs fulfill their potential and live happy lives. My hurt feelings were entirely beside the point.

I dreaded going to class now. It seemed I couldn't do anything right. Irina chastised me like I was an elementary school student. But here I was, a grown woman who knew a thing or two—just not about the subject of dogs (or men, apparently).

I'm not a person who gives up easily so I trudged on, but in the back of my mind I wondered if this process was good for me.

I decided that yes, I was experiencing exactly what every other student in the world was going through. I just had to focus on the fact that I was a student with a very demanding teacher. It also occurred to me that feeling "grown up" can be a trap. As adults, we know things, but we certainly don't know everything. Even if you have a PhD, you might be at a second-grade level in another area of your life.

To learn a new skill, you have to start all over again at the beginning. You have to suffer the start, abandon all the accumulated knowledge that you possess or think that you do. It leaves you with nothing, really, but that's the right place to be when you want to learn.

It's humbling—always a good thing. It's also an uncomfortable state to be in, but I guess it goes with the territory.

Hat's off to all the second-graders out there; I share your pain.

As I buttoned up the loose ends regarding my dogs' health and safety, however, my fear remained. I thought a lot about it. I tried to unravel its source. As I tried to break down exactly what I was afraid of, each concrete thing that came to mind quickly turned into a sparse cloud that, once named, evaporated into the atmosphere. I realized there wasn't an actual "thing" I was afraid of; my fear had more to do with my anxious state of mind and anticipation of disaster or failure. It's not that bad things couldn't or wouldn't happen to me or the dogs, they just weren't happening at the moment. They were happening in my mind—a far worse scenario. It's like suffering for no good reason. I did understand that my fears were mostly irrational and definitely over-blown and exaggerated. But knowing something intellectually is a far cry from managing it emotionally. Consciousness has its limitations.

Since I couldn't quite contextualize my anxiety, I settled on a general plan of action and a point of view—at least with the dogs. As long as I was being as safe as possible, I was doing my best to minimize the potential for trouble. Reassured on that point, I decided to just white-knuckle it through.

The deeper personal issues I needed to confront were set aside. I wasn't quite ready to uncover the truth.

It is wise to pay attention to things that can go wrong—whether in life or with dogs; it's good to be prepared. There is wisdom in that. It leaves you with a sense of confidence that you've covered the bases in case of an emergency. While Irina continued to torment me with all the potentially disastrous things that could happen because of my ignorance, I really did become smarter about how to manage risk and take care of my dogs.

Which is why I began to practice avoidance.

On our walks, Sheila would start growling and barking at the sight of an oncoming dog, so I became a master at avoiding dogs by walking at odd hours and away from places where others walked their dogs.

I learned how to correct Sheila as soon as I saw her ears flip forward or her eyes fix on oncoming prey.

I didn't leave the dogs out on the front porch since they barked at passing dogs.

When the dogs were underfoot and dogging me before dinner, I sent them to their kennels until dinner was prepared.

I became proactive and assertive with the dogs, and they listened.

I carried this same strategy into my life. When I had that butterfly feeling in my stomach, I listened and removed myself from whatever had stimulated the feeling.

This wasn't denial; it was avoidance plain and simple.

If I was anxious about sending out pages of my novel to be read, I'd wait until I was having a calm day to do so. When the phone rang with a difficult client on the other end, I didn't always pick up.

In my personal life, I avoided social interactions that might create anxiety. I turned down lunch dates with acquaintances I wasn't entirely at ease with, and when Henry was being demanding, I avoided him, too. But when you avoid people, there are always consequences: lack of intimacy and connection being the most important ones.

I knew the avoidance strategy with my dogs—and myself—was temporary, but it was all I was capable of.

LOOK AT ME

Sheila can't watch me as she runs the agility course. She either looks at the ground or straight ahead. If I don't position myself properly so she can see me in her peripheral vision, Sheila will just create her own course and take whatever obstacle suits her fancy.

I first noticed this tick of Sheila's on our walks. Robi can look up at me with a smile on his face and keep walking. In fact, Robi has run into more than a few lampposts while happily staring up at me. Sheila believes she can't look up and walk forward at the same time; she can do one or the other. If she looks up at me, she has to sit down. The "look up" and "go forward" option is not in her repertoire. So when I'm running the course with Sheila, I actually have to bend down so that I'm in her eye view. It makes for a sore back.

I tried training Sheila to break this odd habit. I held a cookie up in front of her as we walked to see if I could get her head up. At first, she lifted her head for a few steps then looked down. Then she tried it again for a few steps before looking back at the ground.

Does Sheila think the ground will go away if she stops looking at it?

Nairobi is absolutely sure that the ground is right where he left it when he last thought to look. As a puppy, looking at the ground once was probably enough for him to proceed through life expecting that the ground would always rise up to meet him as he walked.

With Sheila, even a new street is cause for hesitation. *Whoa! This is an unfamiliar place, maybe new rules apply? Maybe the ground behaves differently on this street!*

Limitations are remarkably curious.

At that point in my life, I also did not trust my skills, my experience, or the ground beneath my feet. The actions of "walking the dogs" and feeling "stress free" were not in *my* repertoire. I couldn't watch Sheila take off after a squirrel without imagining her getting killed.

I panicked easily and responded to new situations with fear. I still had to keep checking back to my previous relationships and experiences. Like Sheila, I couldn't keep my head up and move forward.

WHEN IRINA TAUGHT ME THE "look at me" command, I found it to be the most useful thing I'd ever taught my dogs. It's an easy thing to teach border collies, for example, since they are often searching their owners' faces for clues of exciting activities ahead, but my ridgebacks took their time learning this skill. For weeks they looked everywhere *except* at me. Lots of cookies and lots of patience and we finally mastered it. Getting a dog's focus is a powerful tool. When a dog is looking at you, he's ready for work, ready to be led.

I decided to try an experiment with Sheila. On our walks, I started asking Sheila to "look for a squirrel." Her head would pop up, she'd scan the horizon, and if she spotted one, I'd give her a cookie. At first, she was so fixated on the squirrel that she wouldn't take her treat, but eventually she learned to eat *and* look at the squirrel. At first, I felt that I might be doing something subversive—asking her to look for the thing that made her crazy seemed counterintuitive. Turns out, this command signaled a huge turning point in our relationship. When Sheila spotted a squirrel, I'd say, "Good job. Good looking, Sheila." And then I'd give her a treat and tell her to "leave it" and we'd move on. Sometimes, I would see the squirrel first and tell Sheila to "find the squirrel." Her head would snap up wildly, usually in the wrong direction, and I'd tell her "look right" or "look left" or "look up," and when her eyes connected, I'd praise her.

This turned into a hunting exercise. I was training Sheila to spot her prey, not run after her prey. Nairobi followed along with the training, but it was all show. Nairobi doesn't have a strong prey instinct—he has a strong *fun* instinct. So, Nairobi would get all excited on the "look squirrel" command, but half of the time he was really watching Sheila or looking in the wrong direction.

Without realizing it, I was honoring Sheila as a sight hound and giving her work that was suitable to her nature; she enjoyed the game. "Find the squirrel" or "where's the cat?" worked to focus her, and when she spotted the animal, she got a cookie. Nairobi got a cookie because he graciously played along with us.

Using Sheila's instincts gave me more control over her, and it gave Sheila more control over herself. This strategy also worked to desensitize Sheila to squirrel excitement. The more controlled exposure we had with the squirrels, the less crazy she behaved—at least around squirrels.

I wondered what the "look at me" process was in my life. I realized that my daily walk with the dogs was the orienting pattern of my day. For forty-five minutes to an hour, we walked. When I returned home, my mind was clear and alert.

Finding a ritual that grounds you is a valuable tool in life. You can use it to help you get focused no matter what's happening around you. "Look at me" is a return to attention, a reorientation; it's a command that can restore emotional balance and calm an anxious mind.

About ten minutes into our walks—after my anxiety has subsided—we hit our stride. I walk at a fast pace and the ridgebacks settle into their moving trot, which is a natural gait for their breed. We move pretty quickly and then our breathing is deeper, the blood is flowing, and together we get into the zone. I'm not sure what the ridgebacks think about when we hit that cardio sweet spot on our walks, but I "look at me." I examine my thoughts and emotions and check in with myself.

And on those walks, I thought about fear. Why did I imagine disasters? I saw the way Irina approached the dogs, calmly and surely, even when one of the dogs was doing something potentially dangerous. I wanted to react like that.

What was I afraid of?

I finally realized that for me, fear was a symptom of a deep, unsolved, long forgotten equation. It had to do with my right to happiness. Was it a right? And if it was, did I deserve it?

When friends told me they wanted to be happy, I didn't understand what they meant. I never considered happiness to be a priority. Being a good mother, achieving excellence in my work, acting responsibly and honestly, taking the high road, having a good character, giving back, and being kind and loving—these were my priorities.

One of the casualties of a complex childhood is the inability to relate to the cherished belief that one has a right to contentment and happiness. If the message about happiness isn't sent—and reinforced—early on, a child won't expect it or even go look for it.

Families are hard to describe rationally; they are made up of so many subtle details, impressions, and events, all of which are heavily shaded by flawed memory and subjectivity. That said, to me, my family was invested in being, and looking, perfect—and least from the outside. Achievement was prized, talent lauded. Competitive, volatile, emotional, creative, and sensitive, each one of us created a whirlwind of activity on our way to achieving our goals. The word happiness wasn't even in our vocabulary. I don't remember it ever being mentioned in our home. We were encouraged to be the best at everything. This pressure to succeed—to stand out—created stress and anxiety. Our accomplishments seemed inextricably bound to our right to exist. It made for a tense household. To top it off, all of us were outspoken and blunt, and we collided; there were hurt feelings, dramatic monologues, and countless slammed doors.

The youngest of four, I left home, hoping to escape the pressure cooker I'd been raised in, and I promptly began making crucial life decisions without the benefit of good guidance—or good instincts. I simply rushed on. I thought I knew everything at sixteen, but by twenty-nine, it was pretty clear I didn't. Divorced with two children, I believed I had failed at life already. Distraught at where I'd ended up, I simply focused on fulfilling my responsibility as a parent. I locked down my options, and managed what was right in front of me. But the ending of my marriage and the responsibility of taking care of two young children, left their mark; my failure was screaming at me. The dramatic monologues and slamming doors were continuing—just in my mind.

I concentrated on trying harder. I put a lot of pressure on myself to be the best mother, the most responsible professional, the smartest person in the room—the list went on.

The pressure was quite recognizable.

I'd fashioned a terrible trap. I'd been ambushed; I was right where I'd started as a child. My accomplishments, or lack thereof, were defining my life.

Shockingly, this was a surprise to me.

Now what?

To sort it all out, you have to go back to the very beginning; you have to examine the early assumptions you made as a young person and begin to unravel the falsities.

I had never reexamined my early assumption about happiness. I kept repeating my mantra that happiness wasn't important. But the older I got, I think my soul just couldn't stand my mind's nonchalant attitude toward happiness. Time was passing, and it was urgent for me to address where I stood in regard to my expectations of life. So, I believe my inner self was trying to scare me senseless. I needed to wake up to all the joy that was possible in my life and stop hiding behind the pursuit of goals at the expense of myself.

I meditated, breathed, and walked.

There was nothing to be afraid of really. There was only an unanswered question about what I deserved and had a right to. And whether I could—or would—seek it out.

Perhaps Irina intuited the reason for my fear. She never said. What Irina did do, however, was to keep the pressure up. She joined hands with my inner self and put the fear of God into me.

EACH TIME I RESUMED CONTACT with Henry, I gave up less and less of myself and gave more and more goodness to him. I was working something out—about giving and receiving, about loving and being loved. I was still testing "happiness"—whether I deserved it or if it was even important to me.

I think I was also desensitizing myself to Henry. I was trying the "look at Henry" strategy. Each time we connected, there was less friction, less anxiety. I think both of us were losing heart in the chase and were looking for stability, a lessening of the intense attachment that we'd forged.

Between Henry's many houses—I actually forget which one; a fact that is telling in itself—he moved in with me for a few months. Strangely, it was alright. Since he was in my home, he couldn't assert control, and he was respectful. I think he hated it, but I found him to be more gracious than I ever thought possible. I know Henry believed we were going to end up together. While I was doubtful, he thought our breakups and makeups were simply the defining nature of our relationship.

For me, those months that he spent in my home were the most

tranquil in our life together. Even the dogs seemed happy with him. They were excited to see him when he came home. They even wagged their tails. It was as if by being uprooted and disconnected from his touchstones, he became more vulnerable, kinder; he became a man who needed our love.

The only troubling thing during our time together was the fact that Henry didn't offer to contribute to the rent while he was living with me. While I was earning a good living, times were beginning to be tough and an offer to help with the monthly expenses would have been appreciated. I did mention it, and Henry's response was that all his resources were going to the new house. I believe that in his mind, he did think the new house was finally going to be "our" house—once more with less feeling.

It suddenly became clear to me. Henry would always do what was right for *him;* he would never naturally, or even deliberately, do what was right for me. That was who he was. He had always been that way; he was faithful to his nature, and any expectation of a different kind of behavior from him had been pure fantasy.

The important thing for me now was to pay attention to doing what was right for *me.* In the long run, faithfulness to who you are is the greater value. That truth cuts both ways.

Henry was Henry. I finally wanted, needed, and was ready to stand up for—Carol.

I gave up Henry, at least the idea of him. I looked back at our interactions over the years and realized that every exchange between us missed the mark. During our estrangements, Henry had never once picked up the phone and tried to have a conversation with me. It was sad that our life together was mostly evidenced by years of emails. I think Henry was scared to talk to me, afraid to hear what I had to say, maybe even afraid to express his own feelings; yet, he couldn't quite give me up so he maintained the connection, and so did I.

I knew he loved me—I was never in doubt of that. It was a Henryesque kind of love, but it was all he could offer.

What I didn't know was what that love meant to him.

What I did know was that love did not motivate him; it was not a primary force in his life.

More importantly, I was experiencing an awakening about what love might mean to me. As I began to define it for myself, it was clear that my relationship with Henry didn't have the sympathy or kindness or warmth that I needed. His presence pulled the weaker parts of me to the forefront. I had to end that, and for good.

So when Henry moved out of my house and in to his granite kitchen and hardwood floors and landscaped gardens and Japanese soaking tub, I began to disconnect. I lost my fixation. I was never going to fit into his life. I didn't belong there.

I did not want to be there.

IRINA TOLD ME ONCE THAT training a dog never stops. You never get to a point when your dog knows everything and he just does it. Learning always has to be reinforced. Relationships are the same. Life is the same. Work is the same. You can't ever sit back and coast on what you think you know—it's always an effort to keep things moving in the right direction.

I'm not perfect; I never will be. But I will always keep trying.

I knew I had an associated agitation—heightened sensation and excitement—with love. In my heart and in my right mind, I knew that was a wrong connection. When I observed the same behavior in Sheila, I knew it was unbalanced and dangerous.

Sheila was out of control and so was I. Her behavior created a heightened emotional response in me, and not only could she sense it, she was counting on it. Feelings—larger-than-life sensations of fear or panic or anger—aren't to be trusted when working with dogs. They also aren't to be trusted in day-to-day life or in relationships. They obscure reality, and, sometimes, strong feelings can create their own reality. Calm, balanced action and thought were my goals. They seemed very far away.

Sheila and I had an example right in front of us of how to be: Nairobi. He was balanced, loving, generous, with a strong ego immune to attack. Nairobi thinks he's in charge even when he isn't. At his core, he is quite sure of himself and he trusts his experience; he trusts life. Nairobi knows when to back down and leave the field, and he knows when to come out and play. He accepts what's up, doesn't hold a grudge, and he believes he deserves happiness. He expects happiness and he extends his expectation to his pack.

If Nairobi could guide us, he would say, "More cookies. Less talk."

The Course

chapter eight

There were two questions that
plagued me on and off of the agility field:

Where am I?

Where am I going?

I have a terrible sense of direction. I can't read maps or grasp north
and south without pausing to look up at the sun. Even then, I'm
not convinced. I can find my way home, but I can never remember street names. I have found myself occasionally marveling at the
name of a street I have walked for years. *This is Clark Street?*

I intuit my way to places, and while this has worked relatively well
in the real world—especially with the help of MapQuest—it does not
work on the agility field.

In each agility class, you face a brand new course with different
obstacles. You might have a teeter, a tunnel, or a chute (a collapsible

tunnel). There could be a dog walk, a variety of jumps with straight bars or double-bars, or broad or long jumps that cover a horizontal distance. You could find winged jumps, a tire jump, and weave poles. You could also have a table (a low table that the dog has to jump onto, then sit or lie down on for a short pause), an A-frame, or a teeter.

During the class, you might run four different versions of the course.

"Take the white jump, blue wing to the left, take the red wing from the outside, take the tunnel, take the weave poles, take the dog walk, back to the red wing, and finish on the tire."

I walk the course, try to memorize the order of the jumps, and when I think I have it, I go and get one of the dogs. But running the course with a dog is a different experience than walking it.

"Where are you *going?*" Irina shouts as I whirl around on the field, trying to remember which jump comes next.

It's easy to get disoriented while running the dogs. While I'm looking at them, my head is down, and when I finally look up at the field, I'm confronted by a maze of jumps that look very different when I'm smack in the middle of them. My inability to remember the course is a constant frustration. The dogs don't like it either. It's deflating for them to stop in the middle of a course. To them, it must feel like *funnus interruptus.*

At this point in my training, my skills were stronger, which meant that Irina expected more from me. She raised the bar; everything got harder, more complicated, and faster.

Before or after my class, I would watch other students learn their courses and run their dogs without incident. I seemed to be the only student with a bad sense of direction. I winced every time I heard Irina yell, "You aren't paying *attention!*"

I *was* paying attention. I just hadn't figured out how to take a quick picture of the course and keep it in my brain. We all have different learning styles, and I realized that I learn by physically doing something, not by visualizing it. Directions also stick when I repeat the words aloud. If I walked the course, went through the motions while repeating the instructions verbally—and stopped thinking—I could complete the course perfectly. If I just *moved* and *talked*, I could do it. The correct direction was in me; I just had to trust that it was there.

Irina's yelling didn't help.

My frustration and self-criticism didn't help.

I had to shut off thought and rely on my sense memory to guide me.

It's an uncomfortable moment when you understand who you are and how you actually function, especially if no one around you is validating your perception. It's a lonely place, and for me it lasted awhile. I was a pack of one, and the ridgebacks were circling, trying to figure out where I wanted them to go. I vacillated between what I knew would work for *me* and trying it Irina's way.

AT HOME, I NOTICED I exhibited the same disoriented behavior as I did in agility class. When I was confused, I walked around—and thought—in circles. I jumped from task to task and back again. I walked to the kitchen, forgot why I went, moved to the bedroom, looked around, and then went back to my desk.

Confusion is my cardio.

The ridgebacks, being strong pack animals, dutifully followed me. I have a small house, and since I'm tall, and the ridgebacks are big, we often collided in the doorways—we all couldn't fit through at the same time. I'd stop, they'd stop. They'd lean against my legs as if to say politely, "You first? Or should we go?" The sight of the three of us wandering through the tiny rooms must have been an amusing image.

Sometimes I would stop suddenly and I would have a ridgeback positioned in front of me and one behind me. I couldn't move. I was hemmed in by indecision. The ridgebacks were waiting for . . . direction.

Ah.

Direction: Go forward, go back, sit, go to kennel, go to place, or down.

Direction: Find an agent, write a screenplay based on the novel, start another book, find a better romantic partner.

"What's happening with your novel?" Irina asked me one day. "Have you sold it?"

"I'm looking for an agent," I answered.

"How are you doing that?"

"Well, I'm sending out query letters with a synopsis."

"Why?"

"Well, that's the way it's done."

"And then what?"

"Well, I wait for a rejection or a request to read pages."

Irina looked at me as if I was speaking a foreign language. She doesn't really believe in following protocol. She is always looking for the shortest distance to the goal. It's an agility thing, maybe even an Eastern European thing—for sure, it's an Irina thing.

"Why isn't your friend Peter helping you?"

My friend, Peter—the one who had the great beach party that bored Henry to death—is a bigwig in the entertainment industry, and Irina was sure he could help me if he wanted to. I, however, wasn't so sure. I know Peter well, and yes, he is a man who can help when he understands what you need. He's a businessman, and if I had a business, I could ask for advice or introductions. But I needed an agent, someone who believed in my work and thought they could sell it. That's a subjective arena, and Peter doesn't wade into those waters; he's about facts, the bottom line—he's not creatively inclined, even though he's in the creative world. He is a man who could introduce me to anyone I needed to know, but he wasn't the kind of person who would make a phone call for a creative effort. Peter is about things that are verifiable, and art just doesn't fit in there. I understood this about Peter, and I would never ask him to step outside his comfort or knowledge zone to attach his name to a novel of mine; it just didn't fit.

"If he was a *true* friend," Irina pronounced, "he would help you. Real friends take action to help their friends."

Grrr.

I WAS TRYING TO LEARN my course. I was following procedure. I was trying to respect the process.

It was not working. I wasn't in the flow. I knew it. I could feel it. I wasn't stumbling upon serendipity.

On and off the course, I lacked strong and true navigation. And Irina jumped into the role of my navigator.

If I dated anyone new, Irina had an opinion. "Have fun with Jeff, but he doesn't sound like the future for you."

Grrr.

My novel?

"Self-publish," Irina announced triumphantly one day. "Traditional publishing is dead."

Grrr.

I suffered, but I didn't complain—for good reason. Who would possibly understand that my dog agility trainer was running my life?

"THINK LIKE YOUR DOG," Irina said one day when Nairobi kept taking the wrong jump on a complicated course.

Then she grabbed my arm and pulled me down to my knees in front of a jump.

"What do you see?" she asked.

I was irritated. The dirt was hard, my knees hurt. It took me a moment to calm down before I looked at the course. From the position Irina had forced me into, it was clear that Nairobi could only see the jump in front of him, not the jump to the left that I wanted him to take.

"So, what is he thinking?" she asked.

"He should take that jump," I answered, pointing in front of me.

I started to get up, but she grabbed my arm again and kept me in place.

Irina then physically turned me to the left, and now the jump I wanted Robi to take was visible.

"If you angle your approach and use your outside hand to guide Robi, and then your inside hand to indicate the turn, he'll see the correct jump. He'll make the right decision," Irina said.

Oh, I get it. You need to look at the course from the dog's point of view.

"RUN FASTER! YOU'RE TOO *SLOW!* You need to cross in *front* of the tunnel before the dog *exits* the tunnel!" Irina yelled.

I was running as fast as I could, but Nairobi beat me to the end of the tunnel every time. He'd burst out of the tunnel at exactly the same moment that I'd reach the end of it, and we'd collide into one another. There was no way I could manage to run the course the way Irina was telling me to. I kept trying, but it wasn't going to happen.

"Get *ahead* of the dog!"

Oh, I get it. My point of view about the course doesn't matter.

AN AGILITY COURSE IS A very personal thing. It's your skills and physical abilities as well as your dog's. Every agility pair runs a course their own way. There are all kinds of courses, straight and fast, winding, circular, backtracks—every imaginable configuration is possible.

Just like life.

I've always admired people who go straight and fast to their destinations. I guess all those fast and straight people know where they're going. Like Irina. She goes straight to where she wants to go and she always has a plan. She uses navigation in her car, she plans out her lessons, she plans out her life—and to my observation, she is exactly where she wants to be.

At that point in my life, I was surrounded by people who seemed to know exactly where they were going. I seemed to be the only person without a compass. I was stubborn, though. I am like my ridgebacks. I dug in my heels and tried to resist my sense of insecurity. When those feelings rolled through me, I took deep breaths. Irina critiqued my friends' loyalty, the direction I was taking in my career, and my performance on the agility field. My attempts to find a literary agent for my novel were going nowhere. My love life was dismal. More than a few friends suggested I try something else with my life. All around me were fast-course runners reaching their goals. I was all alone on a parallel course and, though I had many days, weeks, months of self-doubt, I simply kept trying.

While I knew my ultimate goal in life (except for the happiness part, which I was still pondering), I wasn't sure of the exact directions to get there. I tried a few routes; every day I seemed to come up with a new plan of attack. When the new plan didn't work, I'd shift gears and try something else. I have moments—okay, days—when I'm dreamy and vague, but I am a creative person. We get that way. While I'm capable of logical thought, I have long stretches of meandering mind activity that may eventually lead to some interesting thinking or writing.

Using an agility metaphor, my life course is like a serpentine, which is an arrangement of obstacles through which the dog's path assumes an S-like pattern. Here's a sample configuration: Three jumps are lined up with a few feet between them. If you start the dog inside the course on your left, the dog jumps away from you and lands to the right, he jumps in toward you on the next jump and lands to the left, and then he jumps out again and lands to the right. From the handler's perspective, you send the dog out with your inside hand, run to the next jump, and call the dog in with your outside hand, then send the dog back out on the third jump with your inside hand. When you perform a serpentine well, it looks like a dance move. This is a forward-moving course, but it is not a fast course. It's elongated, and what might seem like repetition is actually a very elegant way to get where you're going.

But it's slow.

My career had developed along serpentine lines—and so had my love life. In my career, many of my choices were a result of being a single parent. Each career step moved me forward and allowed me to support my children, but I was not on a direct path to my goal. In my personal life, each relationship led me forward, but it was also not a direct route to personal happiness.

What I realized during this awkward time in my journey was that every choice you make—turn left or right, date this man or that one—leads you somewhere. I think I had imagined that I was still getting up the courage to plot a course when, actually, I was already on a course.

I was on a slow, winding, learning course that was taking me here and there. I was sampling along the way. It was *my* course. I had designed it and was continuing to do so. It wasn't a perfect course, but seriously, whose is? While it's possible to edit out the awkward moments in a life for public consumption, all it accomplishes is the perpetuation of the false idea that there is a "perfect" life or way of doing something.

Perfection alienates people. It is attractive, but it doesn't create an authentic, emotional connection. It actually disconnects. It erodes confidence. It preys on human vulnerability. And it's a myth. I was dazzled by perfection almost my entire life. It was pointed out to me as a child: "See how perfectly that artist/athlete/intellectual's life is unfolding! What a story!" And I believed in it—like a fairytale. I never resented the spectre of perfection. On the contrary, I was mesmerized by it. But I did always feel that it was out of my grasp. I would watch a happy family at an amusement park and romanticize them. *They must be so happy!* I'd catch a glance of a couple holding hands, and I'd create a fabulous story around their love. I'd read an article in a magazine about a famous artist, and I'd hold that person up on a pedestal. But I didn't feel connected to them at all. I knew I was imperfect. I'd accepted that from an early age. The competition—and talent—was so ferocious in my family, I hardly even tried to keep pace. And the way my life had unfolded as an adult confirmed my early acceptance of my imperfection. My scrupulousness about my personal deficits, though, created an even bigger chasm between me and those "perfect" people. Eventually, as I matured, I realized perfection doesn't exist here on Earth. It's a trick of the eye. It was never me and them—it was always *us*. Perfection is just good PR. We've all made bad choices, everyone has run an awkward course, and everyone has tripped and fallen. It's simply impossible to avoid the hazards in life, and they come in many forms. Financial hardship, disease, a sick child—not one of us gets off without a taste, or a whole meal, of difficulty. The only thing that binds us together is the commonality of the human condition. Our flaws, our mistakes, our troubles, these are things we should share. They are much more important than our successes. You don't need a crowd around for support when you've done something fantastic; you need people around you when you've fallen and you can't get up. All you need then is one voice in the crowd who says, "The exact same thing happened to me!"

In a way, I was doing exactly what Irina had told me to do; I was thinking like a dog. My nose had picked up a scent and I was following it. I wanted to sell my novel, transition out of advertising, and write full time. I had other books I wanted to write. I wanted to go back to my first love—film—and write a movie. I wanted to find love, not at the expense of my life, but I wanted a love that added to my life. I wanted to be fear-*less*. I wanted to continue being creative, generative, and good to friends and strangers alike. I had goals.

My course was one designed to teach me things I needed to know on the way to getting what I wanted. Yes, I felt vulnerable and exposed on the course I'd chosen, but I was learning. Every day, I had ideas, and during every agility class I made progress. Sheila was still chasing squirrels, but we were working on it. And maybe I was chasing squirrels and windmills, but someone's got to do it.

I was well aware of the fact that I'd designed a slow course. I designed it that way because that's who I am. I'm slow. It takes me time to learn lessons. My learning style requires extra time. Really, I'm a ridgeback—fast when I need to be, and lazing around, working on creative ideas during long sun-dappled gestation periods. I can chase squirrels, and I can sit still for days. I'm a hound-person.

COME FRONT

Early on in our training, Irina taught me three commands: "come front," "come side," and "come heel." "Come front" means the dog sits right in front of you and looks into your eyes. "Come heel" means the dog sits to your left, and "come side" means the dog does the same on your right side. These commands are extremely important in dog agility. You run dogs from both the left and the right sides, so the dog needs to know how to begin the course. During a particular run, a dog also has to be able to function on both sides of the handler. The call to "come front" in the middle of a run also calls the dog in your direction, so that you can show the dog the next obstacle in a tricky course. We practiced these three commands constantly—on our walks, at home, and on the agility field. Every single time my dogs followed these commands, they got a cookie. Because of this, these were the most reliable commands in my repertoire.

When I got lost one day in the middle of the course, Irina called out, "Stand still and call Nairobi to front and then decide where you're going."

"Come *front!*"

Nairobi ran to me with excitement, sat down and stared at me. He got a cookie. And he kept staring at me. I looked around the course, remembering where to go next. I gave him another cookie. Nairobi kept staring at me. I could have kept it up all day—as long as the cookies held out. I had my dog's complete attention while I sorted out where we were going. Why hadn't I thought of this before? I had used the command while running a course, but I had never thought to use the command to collect myself.

It made me think. If you don't know where you're going, just stop. Take a moment. Actually, take as long as you like. Life isn't a race. There's no prize if you reach your goal faster than the next person.

If you've lost your way, stop moving, pick your head up, and look around.

While you're plotting the course, have a cookie—hey, have two or three.

When the course comes back to you—that's the time to get back into the game.

Dogfight

chapter nine

As much as you try to avoid them,
dogfights happen. They are dramatic,
noisy, scary collisions, which is exactly what's
required for a personal transformation.

"Why would a person choose an unbalanced dog?" Irina asked me one day.

You're asking me?

It was a good question, though. In regard to Sheila, I didn't actually choose her, but I certainly wanted to keep her, even after I knew how off-kilter she could be. But when I thought back to my life with animals, I realized I *was* attracted to the crazy ones.

As a kid, I had a summer-long love affair with a very mean horse named Robin. Cleaning his stall one day, Robin bit me on the neck so hard I walked around black and blue for weeks. I loved that horse.

When I took in my Australian shepherd, Cana, as a puppy, she was trouble from the beginning. She nipped at my children's heels, dug under gates and fences, jumped walls, and seemed hell-bent on an early death, which she achieved. I adored her.

Zoe, my favorite angry, neurotic, and needy rescue could not stand any kind of confinement. She'd been abandoned as a puppy and left in a shoe box and had a terror of closed spaces. I made the mistake of shutting her in the laundry room one day, and she tore a hole through the door to get free.

I may appreciate the tough cases, but I'm well aware that they are tough cases. I think many dog owners are in denial about their dogs.

Gosh, sorry that my dog attacked yours. Funny, he's never liked small white dogs.

I don't think my dog actually bit your dog. That was just a playful nip.

Really, he's friendly. I don't know why he's growling at you.

And all of these excuses are usually accompanied by a suspicious look that says, "My dog is *perfect! You* or *your dog* must be the problem."

People not only choose unbalanced dogs, they choose unbalanced partners. We get used to crazy dogs and crazy relationships, and our choices are a reflection of ourselves—of what we love and tolerate. Unacceptable behavior gradually becomes acceptable. Whether it's fistfights in the parking lot or taking off and running into traffic, accepting the unacceptable lets us off the hook. I forgive (or ignore) my dog's or man's or child's unacceptable behavior; therefore there's a good possibility that I can do the same with myself—or they'll do the same for me.

It's a big cover-up: protect the nonsense in our lives and perhaps we'll be spared as well.

But the moment that you accept a certain behavior from an animal—or a person—you have given permission for the behavior. Once you have set a precedent, it's hard to go back.

UNLIKE PEOPLE, DOGS DO NOT like unbalanced behavior in other dogs. They will correct the behavior, avoid the unbalanced dog— sometimes they will even attack. Balanced dogs are quite quick to put a younger or obstreperous dog in its place. When I first started training with Irina, Nairobi was feeling feisty, and he gave one of her male dogs a long, challenging look. Within a few seconds, Irina's dog pounced, had his mouth around Nairobi's neck, rolled him over on his back, and then released him just as quick. And that was that; Nairobi learned his lesson.

While dogs have very efficient methods of stabilizing one another, people do not. We can't go around attacking one another—however badly we might want to.

Where I live, women walk the dogs. I don't know where all the men are. Maybe they have cats. When I'm out in the neighborhood with the dogs, I can tell from a distance whether the approaching pack spells trouble or not. If the dog is straining at the leash, running way ahead of the owner, I know my dogs will react badly, so I book a quick retreat. Weak body posture is another clear signal that the owner isn't in charge. Once in awhile, I run into a woman with total control over her dogs and I am in awe.

For years, there was a woman who walked her dog off leash in front of my home every single day. The dog was a high-energy vizsla that raced past my house. It made my dogs crazy. If the ridgebacks were outside, they would rush the fence, growling and barking. The vizsla owner barely paid attention to her dog or the mayhem he caused. As she walked, she held her head high, her back straight, and she looked directly ahead from behind large sunglasses. Occasionally, she texted on her iPhone as she walked. The vizsla ran ahead of her into the distance, and I could hear all the neighbors' dogs barking as he raced past.

One morning, I noticed that the woman looked like she was gaining weight. The next time I saw her, the swell of her belly revealed that she was pregnant. I actually observed this woman through two pregnancies and she never varied her routine—or put her dog on a leash.

My dogs and the vizsla had their first face-to-face meeting at the beach. Vizslas and ridgebacks look similar. They are copper-colored, and, though vizslas are smaller, you'd think the dogs would recognize that they were similarly proportioned and make peace. Not a chance. I suspect it's an energy imbalance; Vizlas' bark, *Wake up!* and ridgebacks' growl, *Back off!* On this particular day, the vizsla charged, quite close, and barked aggressively. My dogs reacted just as violently. During the encounter, the vizsla owner sipped her coffee and passively watched the scene. She didn't call her dog nor did she say a word as I struggled with my two frenzied animals. Eventually, I got the dogs under control and pulled them away. I was furious.

The vizsla was still barking.

From that first encounter, I made an assumption about who that woman was and what her relationships were like. I imagined she surrounded herself with high-energy, provocative people who raced around her, stirring up trouble. She regarded them placidly, and perhaps that was her power. Like the vizsla who always ran back to her side after causing trouble, maybe the troublemakers in her life ran to her for support. She was both a magnet for, and an instigator of, drama.

Clearly, I didn't like her much.

But I wondered . . . if I was making a snap judgment about her, what judgments were being made about me?

Making snap judgments about people may not be a good thing for humans, but dogs do it all the time. They like or dislike instantly. Dogs also have clear conflict resolution techniques: They fight or posture until there's a winner. It's all about domination. Who's the boss?

People are sneakier. We mind-fight or talk trash behind our adversary's back or walk our crazy dogs off leash—or mention them in a book. Face-to-face conflict is difficult for many of us.

But it happens.

I WAS WALKING THE DOGS on a big, wide street about a mile from my house. I like this street because it gives me a good visual of oncoming dogs. There's plenty of room to turn around and lots of alleys to duck into, should the need arise. As I passed one of the alleys to my right, I saw a very large dog glaring at us from about 500 feet away. Behind the dog, a woman was pushing a baby stroller and talking on her cell phone. Within a split second, the dog began to run toward us. The dog was a young mastiff-mix; the hair on his back was raised, his tail stiff in the air.

"Call your dog!" I yelled to the woman as the dog ran in our direction.

The woman interrupted her phone call to yell back, "He's *friendly!*"

I knew I wasn't supposed to turn my back on a charging dog, but there was nothing to do but try to move my dogs away. We made it to the middle of the street before the young mastiff crashed into my dogs and a fight broke out. I was still holding onto the leashes—I probably should have just let them go—and I was nearly knocked down. The mastiff went for Sheila, and within a few seconds she was down on the ground. Nairobi leapt on top of the mastiff—right on his back. I couldn't help admiring Nairobi's ingenuity. The mastiff had his jaws around Sheila's neck; Nairobi had his jaws around the Mastiff's neck. I finally let go of the leashes and reached for Nairobi's collar.

When dogs are fighting, adrenaline is pumping and awareness is low. If you try to break up a fight, you'll easily get bitten. Your sweet dog won't even know who you are when they are in fight-mode. Grabbing Nairobi's collar was stupid.

I yelled commands—"No! Go home! Go away! Leave it!"—in the deepest, loudest voice I could muster. I'm sure I sounded like an idiot. Eventually, the mastiff disengaged from Sheila and looked dazed.

Clearly, he did not have a plan. For a moment it looked like he was debating the wisdom of taking on two dogs at once. I took advantage of his confusion, grabbed both of my dogs by the collar, and started to pull them away. Unfortunately, the mastiff was inspired to attack again. This time, I was knocked to the ground as the dogs piled on top of one another. It was a dangerous situation. I knew it. I was also aware that I wasn't handling it well. I had no idea where the woman with the stroller was, but I didn't want her near us with a baby. I pulled myself to my feet, dragged my growling and snapping dogs to the opposite side of the street, but the mastiff kept coming. Finally, I yelled, "Get this dog *away* from me!" and a guard at an apartment complex further up the street jumped in her car and raced to the scene, positioning her car between us and the mastiff. I yelled my thanks and got out of there fast.

"My dog is *friendly*," I heard the stroller woman yelling as we walked away. "Her dogs *attacked* my dog!"

Oh brother.

I was livid. How anyone could walk a big dog off leash while pushing a baby stroller and talking on the phone was beyond my comprehension. It was not only selfish, it was dangerous for everyone involved.

Once the ridgebacks and I were around the corner, I checked them for injuries—nothing major. As I was examining Sheila, she gave me a kiss on the face and wagged her tail happily. Nairobi was also feeling pretty damn good. He was puffed up and proud. I think he felt as if he'd acquitted himself well in the fight and had protected Sheila's honor.

Other than a skinned knee from falling, I was fine. I was incredibly lucky that one of the dogs hadn't turned and bit me; it happens all the time.

So, one of my worst fears had materialized and all of us were none the worse for wear. It turned out that I was fully capable of handling the situation, however badly.

Imagining something scary is very different from actually living through it.

It set my mind free; so what if Sheila takes off after a squirrel? If she runs into traffic, the cars will mostly likely stop. If she takes off, the best guess is she will eventually return. Slowly, I began to realize how tightly I'd been holding onto the leash. It was time to loosen my grip. I simply couldn't avoid every probability of danger; I just had to be prepared to meet each situation as best I could.

It's all about calculated risk. You take care to minimize it, but, really, life is a risk. The whole damn thing is a huge risk. Given that, there's no safety in choosing the "right" dog or the "right" man or the "right" job. There's no way to play it completely safe.

There's some wisdom in following your heart, and your nature.

A GAMBLE

In agility competition, there's something called a Gambler's Class. The opening sequence is a timed obstacle run in which the dog and handler complete the obstacles for points. Once that's done, the whistle blows and the "gamble" begins. This part of the competition is also referred to as the "joker" or the "jackpot." In the gamble, the dog has a short amount of time to complete a sequence of obstacles, but at a distance— ten to twenty feet away from the handler. The handler can't step over the line that's been drawn on the field and has to direct the dog over the obstacles from quite far away. If the gamble is successful, the points earned in the first part of the class count.

I don't know how they do it, but the sight of a dog and a handler working in consort some distance from one another is truly amazing. It isn't apparent what connects the dog to the handler, but you can certainly feel the energy that flows between them.

There are two sides to a gamble—you and your dog. You have to trust your dog and your dog has to trust you. To all appearances, the tether that holds you together is nonexistent.

I think that sometimes life seems an awful lot like a Gambler's Class. At points, you are disconnected from your touchstone, your home base—it seems like you're all alone out there—but you have to continue on and trust that what you know will be there for you. You also have to believe that your partner in the gamble will do his or her part and cooperate.

I ARRIVED FOR CLASS ONE day and tied the dogs to a steel post near the field. It was a hot day and Irina was running one of her border collies. This was unusual. Irina has a class before mine, and her dogs are usually in the car. Irina didn't acknowledge me with a hello, which was typical if she was busy. She looked tense, though. I watched her. I could feel emotion emanating from her, and her face was screwed up tight, as if she was holding back a tide of feelings. I thought it might have something to do with her dog, but, regardless, I knew that face and I was sure I was in for a difficult class.

Junior, Irina's youngest dog, was about a year-and-a-half and poised for greatness. Irina's training with him was intense and focused. It was dizzying to follow Junior's course because he moved so fast. Suddenly, Irina moved close to where I had tied the dogs. The teeter was right in front of us, and she began to send Junior over the teeter repeatedly.

When a border collie runs an agility course, it isn't at all like a ridgeback. Border collies streak at terrific speeds; they race; they're noisy; they bang the teeter down; they bark; they might appear, at least to Sheila, like big black and white squirrels.

I began to get anxious. Junior was barking loudly, excitedly, his eyes on Irina—Sheila's eyes were fixed on Junior. And then she did it. She lunged. I took her by the collar and decided to move her back to the car. But then Nairobi joined in with the barking, getting more worked up. Irina kept running Junior close to us, which was making the situation worse. As soon as Nairobi began barking, Sheila's frustration rose and she turned around and bit him. I couldn't believe Irina was running her dog so close to mine. I unfastened the hysterical Sheila from the post when Irina began yelling at me. I could hardly hear her over the barking—I was just trying to get Sheila back in the car.

"Control your dog!" Irina screamed, her voice full of rage.

I dragged Sheila back to the car as Irina kept yelling.

"I can't have you on the field with your dogs! Your dogs aren't safe! My dog could get killed!"

She fastened on that last word with unusual vehemence, even panic. It was unnerving. I was shocked. I hadn't done anything out of the norm. Irina had created the drama. My heart was pounding, and I was surprised to see tears streaming down Irina's face as she continued her tirade.

"Get off the field!" she screamed. "Go home! That's it—we are *done!*"

I grabbed Nairobi and put him back into the car.

With both dogs in their kennels, I stood by my car for a moment. Irina was thirty or so feet away, pacing, her back turned to me. My hand was on the car door. I was ready to leave. As far as I was concerned, she'd behaved like a crazy person—not just crazy, irresponsible. After all her warnings to me about keeping my dogs safe and out of danger, she had deliberately placed her dog too close to mine. It was like she was baiting Sheila. Of course, what happened was bound to happen. Irina had lectured me for years about it—and yet, Irina had instigated this moment.

I have a temper. I don't often show it. When I do, I can be quite dramatic. I was tempted to let loose, to scream back at Irina and tell her what an idiot I thought she was. I was angry. I was in the right—and I knew it.

Then I took my hand off of the car door handle and stepped away from the car. I walked onto the field and stood for a moment. The earth felt solid under my feet. Even though I felt almost light-headed with emotion, I wondered why Irina had behaved so badly. She'd ordered me home, off the field, basically had indicated "I don't want to teach you anymore—I don't even want to know you anymore." *But why?* I watched her across the field, her back to me, and I knew I didn't want to end our relationship this way. I also didn't want to leave Irina with the burden of it ending this way. My pride, my anger, my self-justification told me to get in my car and drive away. But I could feel that my anger was basically meaningless. Irina was suffering with something, and she'd lashed out at me. There was no reason for me to react to her behavior in kind.

It was a gamble; either the bond that this woman and I had forged over the years was strong enough to get us across this hurdle, or she'd lash out at me again. I considered it for a moment, then thought to myself, *Go forward, try to fix this.* I had been so used to reacting to emotional situations, it was a unique experience to decide to *act.* I had perfected the art of the runaway maneuver, and yet here I was, walking toward Irina, now ten feet away. I called out, "Do you really want to end this way?" She began to yell again and I interrupted her. "Is this who you are? Are you a person who throws away five years of training because you're *angry?* Are you *sure* you want to do this?"

I was greeted with dead silence. Then Irina seemed to recover her balance. A minute passed. She took a few steps toward me, looked at the ground, then turned away from me and called out, "Let's start class."

THE RAMIFICATIONS OF MY GAMBLE ran deep. I had turned a corner. No longer chained to an emotionally reactive mode, I knew I was fully capable of controlling a situation and moving it in a positive direction.

I wasn't convinced that I could consistently act on this knowledge,
I had at least demonstrated the capacity for a different kind of response.
I saw that I had developed the inner skills needed to negotiate the confusion of life, love, dogs . . . and Irina. I had worn fear and anxiety as
armor for so long, I felt quite naked in this initiation into calm, capable,
and purposeful. It was as if I'd plunged into an icy bath. It felt good.

THROUGHOUT MY LIFE, I HAVE given up certain cherished things
for my relationships. I suppose we all do. Sometimes it's simply making compromises; you adjust to another's needs and find a middle
ground. But other times, you give up a part of yourself. It's hard to
gauge whether you're yielding to form a compromise or actually being
diminished as a person in the process.

When I played my gamble, when I stood up for myself—and
Irina, too, really—I simply claimed my ground; I took responsibility
for my part of the relationship. I suddenly realized that Irina and I were
equals. She was still the teacher and I was the student, but we offered
an equal amount to one another.

As people, we're flawed. That is an important bond between us. The
challenge is not to let your own imperfection reduce your stature or confidence. You can act with clarity and purpose whether you're perfect or not.

Irina's view of dogs and their owners is unique. She sees them as
more of a collective entity, a democratic alliance rather than a hierarchy.
And she sees the sport of agility as play—true play and cooperation
between man and dog.

"Team play hinges on mutual respect," Irina said one day. "If your dog has to bend over backward to play with you, it's not fair to the dog. He's working too hard. Conversely, if you have to bend over backward to entice the dog to play with you, well, that's like a $50 hamburger. Evaluate what's fair for both you and the dog. Stay within those parameters."

I came to embrace this philosophy not only with my dogs, but with all the people in my life, including Irina. If one person is working too hard, if there's an imbalance, it just isn't worth it. Either establish balance and equality in the relationship or walk away.

Around this time, a new man came into my life—a very different type of man—and I was thrilled. He wasn't Mr. Big; he was Mr. Great. Kind, sensitive, a former college athlete with a razor-sharp intellect, Mr. Great liked to talk politics, spirituality, and literature. He was fun to be around and he was a better cook than Henry! I was in heaven for about three months—before I realized that many things in this man's life just didn't add up. There were also a few long stretches when he was MIA, and I knew that wasn't going to work for me. I stayed in the relationship as long as it worked for me (and a few months more because he was quite irresistible), and then I calmly drew a small line in the sand. When he couldn't honor my modest request, I knew we weren't a fit and I said goodbye. My clarity amazed me.

Of course I missed him. I mourned the loss of his company, which I'd found delightful. He was funny, charming, and sexy. I was sad. But not once did I regret my decision. Mr. Great had turned out to be my $50 dollar hamburger. I couldn't afford him.

LION HUNTING

Dogs on short leashes, cookies in my pocket, I headed out each day for what I thought was a walk. For the dogs, it was lion hunting.

Sheila, in her trademark head-down position, had the nose of a hound and could smell another dog, a cat, or a squirrel from a mile away. From Sheila's eye view, she saw my feet and those of passersby, fences, bumps in the road, front yards, trees, flowers, and her favorites: cats and squirrels. One day, as we walked past a fence we'd passed at least a hundred times, Sheila gave a violent start; her ears pricked forward in alarm, her body stiffened, then she jumped sideways, knocking me off balance. Also alarmed, I glanced at what had caught her eye. There was a shovel leaning against the fence. It hadn't been there the day before. Scary stuff. She could smell and see well into the distance, but she was always surprised by what was right in front of her.

Nairobi walks with his head held high, scanning the horizon for excitement. It could be another dog, a person on a bicycle (maybe they're towing a dog alongside?), a bird, or his favorite: motorcycles! When Nairobi hears a motorcycle, his whole body quivers with excitement and nervousness. Eyes forward, chest stuck out in challenge, Nairobi is ready to charge this metal lion with a loud roar. If he ever got loose, I would expect to find Nairobi chasing a pack of motorcyclists, challenging the shiny metal and leather pride for dominion over his realm.

But here's what happens when we walk: *At first, we move fast so that the dogs can burn off a bit of energy. I run a bit with them, and as we round a corner, I see a pit bull charging in our direction! No, not really. There's no pit bull. It was my imagination. But soon, there's a cat—a real cat—and both dogs lunge. But I have soft hands. I can feel the dogs' tension before they lunge. I grab their collars and turn them away from the cat, or they can sit and "look" at the cat. Either way, I have control.*

The ridgebacks liked it.

As hunters, ridgebacks operate as both sight and scent hounds—whichever works best to track their prey. In their history as lion hunters, ridgebacks were sent out in a pack to track, corner, and hold the lion at bay until the hunter arrived to take his shot. As pack dogs, they are used to hunting in a group, and yet each dog in the group assumes its own unique role without human interference. A pack of ridgebacks is a self-actualized entity; there are the fearless leaders, the beefy middle guys, and those that take up the defensive position at the rear. And they are protective dogs whose second job was to guard and protect their home and family. Essentially, ridgebacks are capable of organically developing a leadership structure. They do their work independently, but they have a fluid response to the pack structure. When I was "on" and assertive, they complied. When I was distracted, Sheila would take over. Nairobi is not interested in a leadership position, but if Sheila was distracted, he'd take over. God help us when that happened. Nairobi would happily lead us off a cliff. He would be smiling all the way down. *Guys! Isn't this fun?*

But my plan was never to be distracted. My plan was to stay engaged—and to play.

Around this time of newfound confidence, I began to say mantras or prayers or positive affirmations—whatever you want to call it—while we took our walks. Really, I was talking to myself, and I must have looked ridiculous, but the dogs responded positively, especially when I included them. At the mention of their names, Nairobi would look up at me with his dog grin, and Sheila's ears would flatten back close to her head, letting me know she was listening. When I finished a mantra/prayer/affirmation, it was the ridgebacks' turn for a self-improvement moment. I'd ask the ridgebacks to "sit," "stand," "sit," and "go," and they would get their cookies. Irina calls repeating "sit" and "stand" in a sequence from the same position "doggie push-ups." The exercise strengthens dogs' hindquarters and goes a long way to toning their muscles and keeping them strong. Nairobi found this talk-walk-exercise scenario hysterical, and every once in awhile he'd jump up and kiss me on the face.

I considered this process active meditation. I wasn't using a book; I was using my instincts. I used my walks with the dogs to verbalize my intentions, to work out creative ideas, to express positive and loving thoughts and feelings. I spoke encouraging words to my sons, my parents, my sisters, and my friends. I solved problems, I crafted stories, and I thanked life for supporting me in all my endeavors. Looking back at this special time in my life, I'd say I was filled with gratefulness for everything I had learned, everything I had, and for all the possibilities that were ahead of me.

Our new ritual helped keep the ridgebacks and me in balance. Random fear had disappeared; in its place I discovered something close to wonderful.

The Way of the Dog

chapter ten

All along,
it was dog wisdom I was seeking.

My dogs are my mirror. They give me a constant, accurate reflection of my emotional state.

Happy? *Okay, we're happy, too!*

Sad? *We'll be quiet and give you kisses.*

Distracted? *Great! Now we can steal food off the kitchen counter!*

Angry? *Oh, dear. If you need us, we'll be hiding in our kennels.*

If there's an emotional vacuum, my dogs will rush in to fill it. If I'm distracted on our walks, my dogs will take over. *Let's go this way!* If I'm holding onto angry feelings inside, my dogs will find a way to express them for me—usually disastrously.

My dogs know me better than I know myself.

Dogs are opportunists. They have learned that by watching us and adjusting to our behavior, they can get closer to what they want—usually, that's food.

There's a certain type of wisdom in a dog's opportunistic nature. It necessitates that the dog be aware, watchful, and attentive to every single thing happening in his universe. People have a harder time accepting observed reality. I know I do. I miss the obvious, the subtle hints, and I can't even read the maps that have been carefully drawn for me. If we took a cue from our dogs, we'd pay attention to what people say and do—not to what we want or *hope* they will say and do.

Comparing dog behavior to our own can be eye-opening. Dogs have so many elegant solutions to life's dilemmas.

You're a big mean dog? Excuse me while I run away!

Ha! I know you! You're the guy who kicked me yesterday. I'm outta here!

When a dog goes out into the yard, he may glance around to see if there's any danger lurking, but once he's satisfied that there are no possums or raccoons or big mean dogs, he'll find a patch of sun and relax. Dogs don't worry about the future, their next meal, or whether their litter mate *truly* likes them.

We worry about everything.

DOG WISDOM

Henry's timing for reaching out to me was flawless: The morning after I'd had a first date, or ten minutes after a professional success, or in the midst of a wistful moment—his name would appear in my inbox. Despite everything that had happened between us, he was persistent. Each time those emails arrived, I responded. Though I was trying to be polite by acknowledging his communications, every interaction with Henry rattled me.

Whether it was a jarring interruption from Henry or trouble at work or some other emotional setback in life or love, I began to rely on dog behavior as a guide to navigate more skillfully through life. I leaned on my dogs—my life with dogs—for support. I watched my dogs carefully, and I saw examples of how I might create more elegant and practical solutions to the stresses in my life. They were sending me messages—and I took them to heart.

Integrity: Just be you.

A dog is who he is. Dogs don't twist themselves into pretzels for us or one another. They live and breathe and sleep (and snore) without apology. They stand their ground or retreat, but it's always dependent on their natures. Dogs can be picky eaters, slow learners, naturally exuberant, or just plain lazy. The only thing all dogs have in common is the unerring talent of being exactly who they are.

I considered my dog-like nature and realized that I am a breed of person as distinct as my ridgebacks. I have quirks, a nature, likes, dislikes, proclivities, and talents. This may seem obvious, but I had spent a good part of my life trying to change essential aspects of my nature to fit in with people or situations.

When I was younger, I trained to be an actress. Fresh from drama school in London, I arrived in New York City ready to take on the world. I enrolled in an acting class taught by the famed actress and teacher Uta Hagen. I was honored to be accepted as her student, but, from the first class, she expected very specific things from me as a young actress. The work was clear. Her training, excellent. Her critiques, fabulous. Uta Hagen, however, did not respect "commercial" acting work. She believed that actors were a special breed and should perform good work written by insightful writers for the higher purpose of illuminating the human condition. Uta believed the role an actor played in society was essential to the well-being of its members.

She did not see the value in an actor doing a breakfast cereal commercial.

If I dared to tell her I'd auditioned for a commercial or a part in a soap opera, she'd look at me in horror, as if to say, "What are you *doing?* that's not acting! That's a corporate job!"

At nineteen, I didn't get it. I thought I was doing what every other young actor was supposed to be doing. Yet, when I'd turn up at those auditions, I'd hear things like: "You're too young, you're too old, you're a perfect ingénue, you're too complex to play an ingénue, you're too fat, you're too thin, you're . . ." and so on. I thought I was being judged by my talent, but really, I'd just stumbled into opinion central.

I tried to twist myself into the image those casting directors thought I was or wanted me to be. Instead of listening to my very wise teacher, I did what I was told; I changed my hair, my looks, tried hard to be "commercial," but with each change I made, I became less and less myself.

I didn't stay with acting very long. The entire process was disheartening. I loved class and I loved performing, but I couldn't digest the judgments being made about me. Frankly, I hated the commercial part of the business and was quite happy to act in a young writer's off-off-Broadway play, but I thought that somehow my happiness was wrong. I was supposed to be chasing success—wasn't I? I couldn't make a clear choice between acting as a business or as an art; I gave the outside world too much power in defining it for me. I should have listened to Uta Hagen; her beliefs about the profession just felt right inside. I should have taken the time to get to know myself and to accept who I was. If I'd done the work then, I wouldn't have spent a good portion of my life trying to fit in where I just didn't belong.

Sometimes it takes some of us a little bit longer to understand the truth that we are who we are. Identity, I ultimately discovered, is not built from approval, success, or acceptance; it's an inner knowledge and faith in one's nature—plus the ability to act on it.

Emotional debt: Don't get into it.

"Go kennel!" I tell my dogs when they've misbehaved. They both lower their heads, sigh, and walk slowly toward their kennels where they curl up and take a nap. Whether it's five minutes or an hour later, the incident is forgotten. Dogs don't hold a grudge.

When I've made a mistake on the agility field and sent my dog in the wrong direction, it hardly matters to him.

When I'm sick and can't walk my dogs, they don't like it, but they don't hold it against me.

This isn't to say dogs don't express their feelings. I've heard many stories about dogs retaliating when they're angry or upset—avoiding eye contact when the owner has left them alone too long or has been on a trip, peeing in the house when they haven't been walked long enough, or even munching on a new pair of shoes—I put all that into the category of "emotional expression." Dogs want to be heard when they're upset with us. But once we've made it right with a dog, he will be more than willing to move ahead from there.

Emotional debt—holding onto negative feelings—is a human construction. Pain, anger, sadness, shame, failure—some of us carry these debts around and randomly assign them to situations that remind us of the original hurts.

Letting go of emotional debt amounts to forgiveness—of yourself and the person or situation that hurt you. In my case, most of the hurts in my heart were from disappointments in my youth and early adulthood. It's hardly fair to make anyone in my present life pay for those. And if I don't let go of the past, it's hard to actually see bad behavior when it's occurring. Emotion obscures reality. That happened to me over and over with Henry. I was so concentrated on my emotional upheavals, I didn't have the clarity to simply correct him when he was being hurtful.

I once went to a Traditional Chinese Medicine (TCM) practitioner for a sore back, and while I was speaking to the doctor through an interpreter (he spoke only Chinese), he kept looking at my face, smiling. I finally asked the interpreter why the doctor was smiling. "He is sending you positive energy," she said. And then the doctor fired something off in Chinese, and the interpreter smiled and turned to me, "He tells you to think happy thoughts. You will get better quickly, just think happy thoughts!"

That might seem like a simplistic solution, but it really worked for me. Changing my thoughts to happier ones and concentrating on the present worked to foster strength and confidence instead of self-pity or resentment.

So, as I think my happy thoughts, I wonder exactly what those happy thoughts are for Nairobi and Sheila. What thrilling images do they conjure up?

I'm guessing it's cookies.

Danger: Avoid it.

Dogs don't usually run headlong toward a known danger unless they are specifically trained to do so. Yes, dogs run into traffic, but it's only because they don't know what "traffic" can do to them. When dogs have been educated that something poses a threat to their welfare, they generally steer clear of it.

My dogs are suspicious of strangers. They sniff around before they accept a new person into the pack. They use their instincts. When a stranger comes to the door, both of my dogs bark, but their ears are back, standing ready to flee should the postman suddenly attack or morph into a wolf. They do not blithely accept new people, situations, sounds, or smells. They respect the unknown.

I live in a crowded urban environment—a California seaside town with equal parts bliss and trouble. Commerce, the ocean, a dense population, and good weather combine to form an invitation for opportunistic crime. One Sunday night, when beachgoers and visitors were trudging to their cars from the beach after a day of too much sun, alcohol, and street performances, I heard crashing sounds in the alley behind my home. I opened the back door to the patio, which is protected by a huge fence, and called out, "Who's there?" The crashing sounds continued. My stomach lurched; I slammed the door shut, grabbed the phone, and called 911. Helicopters soon appeared in the sky overhead. I could see the searchlights streaking over my house, and the noise was deafening. As I spoke anxiously to the 911 operator, both dogs came to my side, sensing my fear; they were anxious, too. A man with a gun had been spotted in the vicinity, said the operator, and police were pursuing him. Suddenly, we heard another crash beside our house as the intruder jumped into the small passageway between my house and my neighbor's.

"He's *here!* He's at the side of my house!" I yelled to the emergency operator.

We heard rustling as he navigated through the narrow space. I was terrified. Sheila ran to the side of the house where the gated door was ajar and gave a low, warning growl as the man snuck by—within a few feet of us. "He's right here!" I cried to the operator. We couldn't see him in the dark, but he certainly saw us—every light in the house was turned on—and he must have heard me speaking loudly on the phone. Suddenly, the man jumped from the side passageway and landed with a heavy thump onto my front porch. My heart leapt in fear. I have glass front doors and the porch lights were on, so the dogs and I could see him clearly—and he could definitely see us. "He's on my front porch!" I yelled. The three of us stood frozen, the phone clenched against my ear, the operator asking me to describe the perpetrator; the dogs and I riveted on the man just fifteen feet away from us. His back turned to us casually as he gauged the floodlights from the helicopters. My eyes went to the latch on the top of the front door, and with a flood of terror, I realized it was unlocked. "Ridgebacks! *Go! Go! Go!*" I screamed, and they both charged forward to the door barking threateningly. The man quickly hopped over my front gate and was gone.

It took me the rest of the night to calm down after this incident, but as I ran the events of the evening in my mind, I could help but notice how differently my dogs and I responded to danger.

My dogs were as scared as I was. They did charge at my command, but they certainly weren't going to if I hadn't asked. They are respectful of threats. They smelled my fear—and the man's—heard the helicopters, and if they'd had a choice, they would have kept barking—and kept their distance.

What a stark contrast from my own response.

First, I opened the door when I heard sounds instead of locking myself in. While I dialed 911, I didn't take a moment to check that the doors were secured. I was relaying the events to the emergency operator, but I could have taken the dogs into my bedroom and locked the door. I was reacting instead of *acting*. I was assertive instead of protective.

I thought a lot about that incident and drew parallels about my response to danger in the rest of my life. I've always regarded danger as a challenge. I chose difficult relationships, work situations, even friends. I had pride in my ability to face up to danger. Many of us throw ourselves into dangerous situations and relationships with hardly a thought. It's as if we don't take ourselves seriously; we're quite casual with our hearts and minds and bodies.

Now, when the hair stands up on the back of my neck, I pay attention. If a situation or person is dangerous to my well-being or state of mind, I avoid it. Danger is a given in life, but accepting it—and inviting it into my life—is not.

Loyalty: Stick to the ones you love—including yourself.

We all know that dogs are loyal. They are the poster children of loyalty. But really, it's more subtle than that. Dogs also demonstrate intense loyalty to themselves. Just because a dog is loyal to you, doesn't mean he'll give up what he wants and needs first. I might call "come!" and my dog may be on his way to me, then see a squirrel, chase it, and then come. He comes—eventually.

If you try to teach a dog a trick, he'll look at you and probably think, *What's in it for me?* If you have a tasty cookie, he just might roll over for you, no matter how strange it might feel to him.

If a dog wants to do something, or doesn't, he'll be quite clear about it. What a refreshing point of view.

If you want your dog to sleep on the floor, but he really wants to sleep on your bed, he'll just wait until you leave the house—and then he'll get up on your bed.

If your dog likes to bark at passing dogs while he's riding in the car, he'll do it, no matter how much you yell at him. Your dog knows you can't control him while you're driving. He figured that out the second time he barked while you were driving and you didn't magically grow arms that could reach back and grab his collar.

If you're ready to feed your dog, he will do just about anything you want in order to get his food. But after his belly is full, all bets are off.

Dogs make clear choices. I think people could learn from their example.

People also have conflicting loyalties. I want to be with you, but another friend called and maybe I should be with her? Then a guy I like just called; maybe I'll just dump you both to be with *him*.

Gosh. That's madness. Make a choice and stick with it. You'll figure the rest out tomorrow.

While dogs essentially do what they like, they also demonstrate an astonishing capacity for loyalty that does not serve their own interests; it serves ours.

Dogs are self-protective, but they will do what we ask. They are bonded to us in an extraordinary way. Just look at dogs deployed in the military or law enforcement—they will go into burning buildings, and take down gun-wielding villains three times their size; it's astounding what dogs will do for us. People who work with these dogs will readily testify to the fact that these working dogs are aware that they are at risk. They are trained to appreciate danger; they feel the stress of working in the field. Dogs may not have the higher reasoning powers to understand death, but they are instinctively coded for survival. Still, they do as they're told.

Why? Dogs believe in us. They rely on us. They depend on us. They know it and accept it. It's a strange bargain dogs and humans struck thousands of years ago, but it's lasted, and it seems to have served both species. We continue on, dogs and humans, side-by-side in companionship, work, battle, and domestic life. I think the relationship will last until the last man and dog are standing.

The night I asked my dog to charge the intruder on my deck was a perfect example of loyalty. I know my dogs did not choose that action. I asked them to do it—for me. They did what I demanded—even though they were aware that they were in danger. That's a powerful dog/human connection and an enormous responsibility. A dog will give up his life for you—if you ask.

That's a loyalty that shouldn't be tested too often.

Risk: Calculate it before you take it.

I have a tendency to jump into situations and *then* look around for possible trouble.

I am the queen of knee-jerk reactions and impulsive responses.

I have many *oops* moments.

My dogs are a little more calculating.

When Nairobi was two years old, he suddenly stopped eating his usual food. I would put down a bowl of kibble, he would look at it, look at me, sigh deeply, and walk away. I, of course, tempted him with other types of food, which he ate gingerly, with great emotion, as if to say, "Well, if I *must.*"

I told Irina about Nairobi's eating problem, and she didn't hesitate with her answer: "Put the food down, give him a minute to take it, and if he doesn't eat it, take the food away until the next day."

Seriously?

"But won't he starve?" I asked, a little concerned.

Irina laughed. "When he's figured out that he isn't getting better food than that, and he's hungry enough, he'll eat."

I followed Irina's instruction, and the next time Nairobi looked mournfully at his dinner bowl, I took it away. He went to take a nap. This struggle lasted for two days. Well, really it was my struggle. Nairobi didn't seem any worse for the wear. He was his usual happy self—until dinnertime. He sent me long, sad, highly meaningful looks, but they weren't frantic. He communicated profound disappointment . . . and I resisted.

Magically, on the third day, Nairobi ran happily to his bowl of kibble when I put it down and ate hungrily as if it were his favorite dinner imaginable. It took Nairobi approximately forty-eight hours to accept that the stakes were high . . . and he gave in.

Like people, different dogs have different risk thresholds. Ridgebacks are bred to go without food or water for long periods of time because of their life and work in an arid climate, so going on a two-day fast to get tastier food wasn't much of a risk. Once it was clear the food wasn't getting any better, the gamble was over.

In agility, Sheila always calculated risks: Chase the squirrel and risk the loss of cookies and my disapproval? Worth it?

Working with my ridgebacks has given me an appreciation of risk, and my own tolerance for it. If I want something, I have to be willing to take a risk to get it—and then I have to accept the consequences if it doesn't work out. For me, that means everything from walking up to a cute guy I meet at a party or sending out pages of my writing work to members of a neighborhood book club to get their opinions. I could be rejected on both counts, but the gain has to outweigh the effort. Conversely, I've learned that some risks are just too dangerous or require too much effort for me to take. Responding to a sexy email from Henry or agreeing to work on a project with a demanding client who always paid late—if at all—was tantamount to stupidity.

Carol, don't do it!

I have options. I don't have to jump at everything that comes my way. Sometimes I can take a pass . . . or wait for what I want. In the meantime, I can always go take a nap.

Responsibility: Accept it.

When a dog has done something wrong (at least in its owner's eyes), he won't argue his case. A dog might even alert you when he's made a mistake by skulking in the corner and acting guilty. A dog will look straight into your eyes, as if to say, "Yes, I ate the couch. I'm terribly sorry. I don't know what came over me. No treats tonight, right?" And a dog takes his punishment like . . . a dog.

When Sheila has done something wrong, she doesn't wait for a reprimand; she puts herself in the kennel. Nairobi hangs his head low, pleading for forgiveness.

Dogs can't possibly understand the concept of responsibility. It's a complex ethic to grasp—even for people. Yet dogs act in a responsible manner far more reliably than their human counterparts.

It's hard owning up to a mistake, a blunder, or even outright bad behavior. I struggle with this. My pride occasionally overrules my good conscience, especially if I say something blunt and unkind without really intending to.

Really? I said that? Are you sure?

On a larger societal level, frank apologies seems to be missing in epidemic proportions among people who should be setting good examples. Politicians or corporations—it seems rarer these days to hear "I'm so sorry" or "you're right" or "I behaved terribly, please forgive me."

Dogs just get it. They get their part in the if-then consequences of their action. Dogs are masters at contrition.

A dog's acceptance of responsibility, however, only applies to "now." If too much time has passed between the action and the discovery, a dog won't have any memory of wrongdoing. I like this. While I try to take responsibility for things I've done wrong, I think there should be a moratorium on past mistakes. For me, accepting responsibility should take place at the very moment when you've done something wrong. It takes discipline to point out a problem you're having with someone while you're having it. It's gracious to let go of a past hurt when you've failed to point it out.

It's also smart.

Forgiveness is far more satisfying to the "forgiver" than the forgiven. When you let a hurt go, you're free.

Joy of Life: Have it and trust it.

Dogs know how to have fun, how to survive trauma with tail wagging, how to mourn lost loves and welcome new ones, how to enjoy food and tolerate the lack of it, how to chase a squirrel into a tree and not be the least disappointed for not catching it, and how to curl up for a long nap when a patch of sun appears.

It may be our world, but it's a dog's life.

"TO A DOG, AGILITY IS RUBBISH," Irina said one day.

"What do you mean?" I asked.

"Jumping over obstacles and going through tunnels doesn't mean much to a dog. A dog might do it if he had to, but it hardly makes sense. The only reason why dogs do agility is so that they can play with their owners. It's fun. And if there are lots of cookies and laughter, a dog will take jumps and go through weave poles for you. If you get a dog on board, he will do just about anything for you."

Fun . . . Fun!

What a marvelously simple concept; if it's fun, it's possible. This applies to life and business—but also to how we think about ourselves. To be truly effective, you have to believe in what you are doing. You have to get on board with yourself. No self-criticism and no tough love. Only an enthusiastic, positive state of mind will help you get from A to B. If negativity and self-criticism worked as a life strategy, I'd be all over it. But love, joy, and an appreciation of life and its gifts truly works better.

And fun works best.

Capturing the joy in life on a day-to-day basis came late to me. Worry, anxiety, and fear were barriers to my appreciation of life's goodness. My dogs turned me around on this subject. And all I had to do was watch them . . . and play with them.

Playing with my dogs in agility showed me how sheer enthusiasm and the expectation of a good time are powerful motivators. Playtime should be mandatory for adults. We should all have recess once a day—and play hard. How wonderful it would be if corporations had playgrounds, and employees got to play on slides, swings, and the monkey bars. Boardrooms would be filled with better decisions—and after work, bedrooms might be filled with more lovemaking.

My dogs trust me, but they also trust life. They act as if life will provide for them. Call my dogs naive, but that trust is wise. Doubt and anxiety only lead to more of the same. Having a positive attitude—or "acting as if" life will deliver wonderful things to us—at least primes us to recognize and search for those good things. And better, it helps us cultivate it. Of course, life is filled with tragedy, in spite of a positive outlook, but expecting the worst just prolongs the terrible feelings. This is something that I'm learning—to trust that life will take care of me. Worry or concern doesn't make me any happier or life more responsive or supportive of me. When I think back on my life, I've always been supported by opportunity, chance, love—and dogs.

I choose to trust that it will always be that way.

IRINA AND I WERE TALKING about this "joy of life" concept one afternoon. We'd just had lunch and we were standing in the parking lot next to our cars.

"Imagine that it's raining," Irina began. "We could scurry into our cars to stay dry and race home. You know what dogs would do?"

"What?" I asked.

"Stay and play," she pronounced.

I laughed.

Irina is like Nairobi in spirit; when I laugh, she keeps going.

"So, it's raining and you and I have no umbrellas. You know what we could do? We could splash around and play in the puddles."

I giggled.

"We could dance around, shock everyone—just choose to have some fun."

It was true. We're presented with so many opportunities for joy in life that we don't take. Rain, snow, even a flat tire, can all present chances for fun. A dog can have fun anywhere, any time; it all comes down to a state of mind.

If you look for fun, it will usually show up.

Signals: Give the right one and everything will be clear.

If a dog is hungry, he'll let you know. Dogs yelp when they are injured, they look miserable when they're sick, and they get excited when they want to go for a walk. Dogs are quite clear about their emotional and physical states. They are incredible communicators.

If your dog acts happy, he is.

As we enter the world as infants, we, too, are great communicators. Even without words, babies can tell us when they're hungry, in pain, or happy and contented. As we grow older, however, we develop a more subtle manner of communication: the mixed signal.

Do you really think I look good in this dress, and if so, why are you making that face?

Did you like the dinner I just made or did you secretly give it to the dog who looks awfully happy right now?

If you liked me as much as you say you do, shouldn't you be returning my calls?

Our refusal to send clear signals is confusing. It's hard to know how anyone really feels about anything. Unfortunately, most of us are drilled from childhood to be polite, and the truth gets lost somewhere along the line.

A man I've known for years once asked me if I was open to a romantic relationship with him. I had the perfect opportunity to tell the truth, which was a resounding *no*. I believe I said everything but that.

When Henry and I were living together in "our" house, I did not express my unhappiness clearly. Rolling my eyes in exasperation or keeping my mouth shut does not qualify as good communication. If I'd sat him down and expressed how alienated and unhappy I was, at least Henry would have known where he stood.

If I give the right signals, I'll never catch anyone unexpectedly with the truth.

I'm working on this.

ON THE AGILITY COURSE, DOGS look to their handler for direction; they need clear signals to tell them where to go. The map of the course is in the handler's head; the dog hasn't a clue. I saw a wonderful photo of a ridgeback running a course at an agility trial, and in the picture, the dog is mid-air over a jump, body forward, head turned completely to the side, looking into the eyes of his handler as if to say, "Where do I go now?"

In this case, the wrong signal or a confusing signal could have gotten that dog hurt.

And when you think about it, all wrong signals have the potential to hurt in one way or another.

Clarity is kinder in the long run.

Friendship: Be a member of the pack.

My dogs wouldn't think of embarking on a task, an adventure, or even a sojourn outside the front door without company.

Not only do my dogs enjoy company, their behavior is always consistent. They are nonjudgmental, affectionate, responsive, and cheerful. I've never seen my dogs in a bad mood. What a perfect example of the demeanor and attitudes required to be a good friend.

Since it's a dog's natural state to be a member of a pack, the species models an interdependent social structure. Dogs don't like physical distance from the pack, and they are crazy with joy, curious, and sometimes even suspicious when a pack member returns safely to the fold after a solo jaunt. In a perfect dog world, every pack member would be cuddled up, piled on top of one another for warmth and safety, or heading out into the world in a large, forceful group.

While families and friends are our versions of packs, society romanticizes loners and certainly encourages independence—as if the more alone we are, the stronger we are.

This is kind of an odd way to move through life, though I've certainly attempted it for long stretches. And a dog would think of a lone pack member as vulnerable, possibly weak, and sick.

I've always been a solo operator, but the wisdom of having people to rely on in life has not been lost on me. I've found this to be the most important lesson I've learned from my dogs, though I was slow to incorporate it into my life. I now make an effort to reach out to family and friends on a regular basis, but the biggest change I've made is asking for help when I need it. This was a difficult thing for me to learn, but it has brought me much closer to my pack—and them to me.

And once I got a taste of the goodness of being firmly ensconced in a supportive pack, I couldn't imagine living any other way.

It's intelligent to bond.

Belonging makes you strong.

Relying on others creates connections.

And maneuvering through life with a pack is a whole lot more interesting than trying to go it alone.

Gratitude: Always say thank you.

Nairobi and Sheila have many ways of communicating their gratitude—all day long. They look at me with adorable expressions for no reason at all. Sheila is a master at this; when she catches my eye, her eyebrows knit with emotion. Both dogs give me kisses after I've scratched their ears, their tails thump happily when I rub their bellies, and they look grateful when they get a cookie or a nice meal. When we're on a walk, Nairobi always looks up at me with his head tilted, mouth open in a happy grin as if he's saying, "Thank you!" My dogs express gratefulness.

This is a very simple concept, but it was one of the hardest for me to see. I wasn't aware of my ungratefulness; I didn't think about it. Of course I said thank you to friends, family, and to others as I went about my day, but I was not in a state of gratefulness. Thanking the Creator—or even life itself—for every day I received, for all the beauty and goodness that was delivered into my life, well, that's just good manners. When it suddenly dawned on me that prayers of thanks were more respectful than prayers of need, the tumbler clicked in my mind.

This was a simple shift for me to make, but its impact was significant. I found that when I was grateful, mysteriously, more goodness appeared. There are probably countless reasons for that, one of them being that I simply paid more attention to the gifts already in my life, but the fact is, "thank you" is a powerful expression. It transforms what you see. It may even determine what you get. It definitely shapes how others experience you.

Respect: Here comes the sun, my *everything*.

Nairobi likes to sunbathe. It's his first thought when he wakes up each day: He rushes to the porch door, knocks it with his paw, nudging me to open it so he can lay on the deck in a warm patch of sun. *Sun!* He does this all-year-round, every day. In the winter, I suspect he needs the sun to warm up his bones. I have no idea what possesses him in the summer when it's blistering hot outside. Maybe he has some glimmering, genetic code memory of Africa? Whatever the reason, Nairobi is a dedicated sun worshipper.

One day, I let Nairobi out onto the porch and I went to make coffee. After a few moments, I heard a loud, demanding bark from him.

"What?" I called out.

He ran back inside with an intense look on his face. "Hey, *you!*" he seemed to be saying.

"What's up, buddy?"

He barked again. He was *mad!*

I didn't have time to figure out what was bothering him so I ignored him, but I noticed that one or two days a week, Nairobi would bark at me. He was trying to tell me something.

Nairobi's frustration with me increased over the next few weeks, and one day, he must have decided that he had to dumb-it-down for his not-so-bright owner. He ran to the front deck, looked at the slats of wood, looked at me with an indignant expression, his head cocked, ears taking flight, and he barked. Then he ran to the back patio, looked at the ground, then at me, and barked again. He repeated this twice. I could not figure out what he wanted. Then it dawned on me; he wanted the *sun*. I began to laugh so hard I cried. It was cloudy outside and there was no sun! Nairobi thought I was responsible for that hot glow and I was withholding it from him.

Amazing.

When I relayed the story to Irina, she told me, "To dogs, we are everything. We bring the sun, food, love, and access to the world. People are the gods in a dog's universe."

If we're the gods, poor dogs.

I was cooking dinner for Nairobi and Sheila one evening, and I took a phone call. I put a half-cup of kibble along with their supplements into their bowls and dinner was served. Distracted, I forgot the meat that was sitting in the frying pan on the stove. As I was talking, the dogs wolfed up the kibble. Nairobi finished and looked up at me with a big question mark on his face, those amazing ears of his flying out in alarm. I was still talking so I didn't pay much attention to him. In the next few minutes, Nairobi ran to the stove, pointed with his nose, and then back to me with an earnest look. He did this four times before I put it together. *I forgot the meat!*

How wonderful that dogs behave so graciously, considering their relative helplessness in this world that we've co-opted them into.

How cool that they persist in their attempts to communicate their needs to their "gods."

Wow.

I have not gracefully or graciously accepted my helplessness or lack of control, and I am not persistent about making sure that I've been heard.

Got it.

A Clean Run

chapter eleven

*When a dog runs a course without any faults,
it's called a clean run.*

*In life, it's impossible to avoid faults.
Moments of unobstructed speed, advancing
toward a goal—these are the human
equivalents of a clean run.*

The very moment that things began to come together for me, they fell apart. I'd never felt more comfortable in my skin, but life tested this newfound confidence. As everything falls apart, though, it often comes together again in surprising new ways.

AFTER SHEILA'S ILLNESS, I KEPT her on prednisone for over a year, gradually tapering her dose down until she was taking two milligrams every other day. Even though she'd gone through the holistic protocol and was on a maintenance regimen, I held onto that last prednisone dose like a lifeline. For me, those two milligrams stood between life and death for Sheila.

I took Sheila to her original veterinarian for a checkup and put her through a battery of tests. I was hoping that her high ANA (anti-nuclear antibody) titers (level of concentration), which had originally signaled her disease, were normal. It was a fantasy of mine; my dog had been miraculously cured.

While her original diagnosis was immune-mediated polyarthritis, I'd seen SLE (systemic lupus erythematosus) on her chart, which was an even more severe diagnosis. For both conditions, the cause is unknown, but the dog's immune system produces antibodies against the dog's own tissues, reacting to them as if they were foreign invaders. This creates an inflammatory reaction that can affect the joints, skin, muscles, kidneys, blood and blood vessels, heart, and other organs. It can also affect the skin, resulting in ulcers, rashes, dermatitis, crusts or scales, and hair loss.

Sheila had experienced it all. But for an entire year, she hadn't shown a single symptom. *Maybe it was gone?*

The doctor was surprised to see Sheila looking so well. He checked her smooth, pain-free gait, noted her shiny red coat, well-developed muscles, and even though she was shaking with nerves, he couldn't believe how healthy she looked.

"She looks like a different dog," he said.

I explained her holistic treatments and he was supportive and curious.

"Let's see what the blood tests show, but really, she looks great."

He looked down at the chart and saw that I was still giving her prednisone. "You can stop the steroid," he said. "Two milligrams doesn't have any effect on a dog of her size."

I felt a sudden panic. "Are you sure?" I asked.

"It's not doing anything for her." He saw my fear and smiled. "Really, she'll be fine if you stop giving it to her."

I left the hospital amazed and stopped giving Sheila the prednisone that day. I watched her like a hawk, but each morning that she woke up without pain, I was reassured.

A week later, I got a call from the doctor. Her ANA titers were still elevated. She still had the disease, but based on her behavior and his exam, she was in remission.

"Should I be doing something else?" I asked.

"No," he answered. "Continue on with your routine. It seems to be working. Enjoy her."

We were saved—and not.

IT'S A BLESSING THAT TIME softens the edges around a painful event. Sometimes it's even entirely possible to forget an agony from the past, but it's always there, really. The feelings just take a rest; they're on pause. Trauma is never really forgotten, just temporarily unremembered.

I was walking the dogs on a Sunday morning in the middle of summer. It was a very hot day, and we'd taken a long walk; both dogs were tired. We'd reached the alley behind our house and as we turned into it, a woman with a terrier walked toward us. Sheila strained furiously against her collar and barked; she was filled with rage—unusually so. The terrier responded, Nairobi chimed in, and I pulled the dogs past the woman and her dog. I was concentrating on the dogs when Sheila looked at me, startled. A flicker of fear flashed in her eyes, and then she collapsed to the ground, her body shaking with violent seizures. Nairobi went crazy and immediately tried to pounce on Sheila. Either her out-of-control movements or the scent she was emitting triggered his attack mode. Terrified, I tried to hold back a crazed, aggressive Nairobi while also trying to soothe Sheila, whose body was wracked with convulsions.

"Oh no, no, no," I cried. "Please *no!*"

In that moment, I was certain she was dying, and terrified that Nairobi would savage her last breaths from her if I couldn't pull him away. My thoughts were spinning crazily. I didn't want to leave her alone, but I had to deal with Nairobi. Sheila continued to convulse and then urinated on herself, foam bubbling from her mouth. It drove Nairobi mad.

There was no one in sight to help, but I didn't have a voice to call out. I was hoarse with fright. I dragged Nairobi to the house, pulling his frenzied eighty pounds to the back gate. I shoved him through the door and ran back to Sheila. He threw himself against the back gate, nearly shattering the wood.

I fell to the ground next to her, stroking her softly, and spoke soothing words. "You're okay, beautiful girl. I'm here. It's gonna be alright. Stay with me."

In that moment, as I felt her vibrancy eclipsed by a foreign invader, her body seizing uncontrollably, every horrible, sad experience that had ever happened to me funneled through Sheila's convulsing body. It's strange how a dramatic event can channel emotional experiences from your past. Witnessing another's suffering, it's your own sadness that can dominate. My own life came to the forefront: the remains of long-ago troubles; memories of a past that I hadn't let go: romantic heart-breaks, guilt, failure, disappointing those I loved . . . my baby's first skinned knee; I remembered it all.

The seizure lasted for four minutes.

And then, just as suddenly as it had started, it stopped. Sheila's eyes popped open, and she immediately struggled to stand. Her tail wagged, and she looked embarrassed, even ashamed. She was woozy and collapsed several times, but her tail kept wagging, and she was delighted to see me, trying to leap on me and cover me with kisses as if I'd just come home from a long trip.

Oh my God! My relief and worry butted up against each other as I carefully guided Sheila home, my own limbs tremulous from the dissipating adrenalin.

I managed to get her inside the house and quickly kenneled the hysterical Nairobi. I was afraid he might kill her.

I grabbed the phone and called my holistic vet at home.

"Marc," I said, my voice sounding small and distant to my ears—and then I burst into tears. "Sheila had a seizure. What *happened* to her?"

Marc didn't waste any time and immediately ordered instructions, his voice calm and direct. "Wet a towel with cool water and wipe her down. Put the towel on the pads of her feet."

"Okay, okay . . ."

I ran to get a towel and did as instructed. My hands were shaking.

"Now, take her temperature," he added. "You need to see if it's elevated."

I searched through the cupboard, but couldn't find the thermometer. I started to cry again.

"Carol, stop crying. Find the thermometer. And keep an eye on her just in case she has another one. Seizures can come in clusters. How long did the seizure last?"

"Four minutes . . . Marc, she's pacing and stumbling around."

"She'll be all right. Just take her temperature."

"Okay, okay . . ." I frantically pushed through the Band-Aid boxes and cold and flu remedies, trying to find it.

"My dog, Buzz, had a seizure several years ago and never had a recurrence."

"What caused it?" I asked as I pushed to the bottom and saw the telltale clear plastic tube and inside the silver tip of the thermometer.

"Not sure. It's not that uncommon for dogs to have seizures."

With the phone squinched between my ear and shoulder, I gently held Sheila still as I took her temperature. She was panting and swaying.

"Marc, it was hot outside. Could she have been dehydrated? Could that cause a seizure?" I was grasping at straws, wanting an answer that wasn't tied to disease.

"It could, sure. What's her temp?"

"I had them out for an hour. Maybe it was too long?"

"What's her temp, Carol?" he repeated calmly.

"Uh . . . 99.5."

"Okay, that's good. Hydrate her. Keep the pads of her feet wet and cool."

I started crying again—all my pent-up angst about losing her over the last year, like I'd been holding my breath, got the better of me, and I simply couldn't form words above the emotion. Marc listened for a minute and then spoke to me in a strong, soothing tone. I'm not sure exactly what he said. "Breathe" may have been the magic word that settled me. I was to watch for more seizures, but the longer she went without another one, the better the prognosis. He instructed me to take her to the vet and have her blood work done. Perhaps she'd developed epilepsy, he explained. Maybe she had a seizure disorder. It could be a brain tumor. Or maybe it was an anomaly, an unexplained seizure.

I thanked Marc and hung up the phone.

And then I hugged my dog.

It was too much to digest, but of course, I did. One hour turned into two, then four. I bathed her to get the smell of urine off her, and within five hours, Nairobi had calmed down enough to be in the same room with her without trying to attack her. Sheila kept looking at me. *What happened?* she seemed to ask.

I don't know.

That night, Nairobi and Sheila snuggled up together on the bottom of my bed. I stroked them both and sent out silent prayers.

The next day, I took Sheila back to the veterinary hospital for tests and a few days later the blood work came back. Her organs were functioning. White and red cell blood counts were fine; we were back to normal.

Her seizure was a mystery.

Saved—but not.

IT WAS A WAKE-UP CALL, a reminder that life is never perfect—and it's ephemeral.

As good as it gets, it's a temporary situation.

Dogs can put us in touch with this reality. I'm not sure if it's their innocence or vulnerability or how dependent they are on us, but when a dog is suffering, it immediately puts you in touch with the fragile, transitory nature of life. A dog's life is a relatively short one. Anyone who's owned a dog has experienced loss. We outlive our dogs. Some of us are there for our companions' last breaths; others stumble unexpectedly upon their cold, stiff bodies—shock and heartbreak in equal measure. A dog's death is a profoundly sad experience, and yet, all of us dog lovers sign up for the experience. It must mean that the gain of a dog's presence in our lives outweighs the eventual pain of losing him. Or it could mean we need dogs to teach us to appreciate every single moment of life—before we truly lose it.

Here, dogs are the masters.

Just wake up.

Pay attention to the good stuff, deal with the bad. It's an unsigned contract we're bound by; if you want to live, you have to accept life's terms. It seems simple; it *is* when everything is going well. When we're shocked out of complacency, that's when faith and determination are tested. For those of us who vacillate, who have an unsure relationship with our place in life, every test is an opportunity to believe. Every traumatic event, big or small, is just another chance to take an option on the "life deal," to assert a contextual framework that declares: This is *all* worth it.

CONTACT

In agility, there are obstacles that require dogs to touch a safety zone with their paws. Dog walks, teeters, and A-frames all have safety zones. These are "contact obstacles" that have yellow painted strips to designate the spot where the dog must make contact. A "missed contact" is the failure to touch the yellow safety zone while dismounting the obstacle. Missing a down contact zone is faulted under all agility rules.

When Irina was training the dogs and me, we learned the "touch" command. It begins by placing a small cookie-filled cup on the ground at the bottom of the obstacle. As the dog descends and reaches the yellow area, the dog stops and eats the cookies while you say "touch." Often, the touch command is reinforced with a clicker. Dogs pick this up fairly quickly, and soon you can call "touch" even though the cup is empty. The dog "touches" the cup with his nose and then you can drop the cookies in the cup. All the touch command does is get the dog to slow down on the contact point. Dogs see black and white clearly, but their vision is less distinct when it comes to colors. Cookies clear up any possible confusion; you can use their noses (and their hunger) to get them to stop on it.

Hitting the yellow zone while ascending or descending an obstacle like a dog walk or a teeter is important. It's not just for the judges; it's for the safety of the dog. Pausing on the contact zone means the dog isn't jumping off the obstacle midway up or down, which is potentially dangerous. The contact is a safety zone for the dog. It's also a chance to get the dog to look at you and reconnect in the middle of a run.

Nairobi learned the touch command at a young age, and he will touch my face, hand, foot, and the floor on command. Occasionally he doesn't wait for a command. He has poked his nose in a "touch" while I've been holding his food bowl, knocking his entire dinner to the floor.

Oops.

Sheila loves the contact on the dog walk. It took her so long to learn the dog walk, she now adores this obstacle and is reluctant to leave it. When she climbs down the dog walk and hits her contact point, she sits—happy to get her cookie. If she sits long enough, maybe she'll get two or three. Sheila is clever that way.

Contact points are chances to reconnoiter. When you don't hit them, there can be casualties.

It happens in real life, too.

THE BUSINESS CLIMATE WAS difficult, but for my advertising clients, it was dismal. One-by-one they cut back on their budgets. The business I'd built so carefully for ten years was threatened.

My personal relationships went through the same transition. Every tentative, built-in-the-sand connection began to fall away. It was as if life as I knew it was beginning to disintegrate.

External reality does not bend to personal will. It flows along despite our grand moments of illumination. Life is like Irina: forward-moving, demanding, occasionally irrational, but always educational.

That said, I looked at my dwindling business and realized that I had stopped hitting my contact points. Those safety zones that are so important in life and in a career have to be "touched" so that in times of trouble you have some support, something to turn to. Friendships can be contact points, and for me, writing is an important one. When I am coming up with ideas, forming them into stories, developing new projects, it keeps me safe; it creates my future. There's no coasting on success in this life.

My response to this dramatic turn of events in my career was simple: I walked the dogs, I trained in agility, I wrote and created new projects. I filled the empty spaces with creativity. I entered the most creatively fertile part of my life. Instead of reacting to outside noise (life can sometimes feel a lot like Irina yelling at me), I turned inward. Years of agility training taught me that a steady application of energy and action—plus rewards—works better than anything to get things back on track.

Setbacks can be disheartening. I remembered back to previous times in my life when I was faced with difficulties, and while I always trudged on, I did so with anxiety and panic just under the surface of consciousness. Failure wasn't an option, but I still feared it. This time, however, failure didn't occur to me. One of the results of training, for people and for dogs, is that you build resiliency. Practicing right action and good thinking has a clear result. *Right action and good thinking.* I'd worked hard toward a goal and the effort had paid off.

I studied what was happening in my professional field and realized that traditional advertising—the way I'd been practicing it for years—was changing. There were new techniques and tools available for clients—blogs, social media, online communities and networks—and I decided to learn them. While I'd been holding the fort, there was a whole new world out there. It was time to go introduce myself.

In my writing life, I turned toward nonfiction. Early on in my career I'd worked on some nonfiction projects, and I hadn't felt it was a fit for my skills. But the literary climate had changed. There was a wide range of voices in the nonfiction world, new storytelling trends, and many interesting authors. It was an appealing environment. I decided to chime in.

Agility was just as demanding, but strangely, I was getting quite good at it. It became my refuge. While I knew I'd never master the sport, I did find myself at a point where I was facile—a word that sometimes brings tears of joy to my eyes when it applies to my efforts. Needless to say, since I was doing everything right, Irina had little to complain about. That led to an absence of yelling.

Yay!

WITH THE DOGS RUNNING AT their peak, going to class was a pleasure. Nairobi jumped high and ran fast. Sheila was gaining ground on her cousin, running smartly and aggressively. She'd turned into quite a competitive dog; she wanted to be *better* than Nairobi, and she tried hard to excel at every turn. Her happiness was palpable, and though I had moments of anxiety about her health, her stamina on the agility field was phenomenal.

The day that I saw how far we'd come was entirely ordinary. We turned up for class. It was early spring and there was a chill in the air. I ran Nairobi first. It was a fun, demanding course—lots of twists and turns. Next up, Sheila. We ran the course once and she flew over the jumps. When Sheila is happy, she smiles; she lifts the sides of her mouth in a grin. It's subtle, this small smile of hers, but when I see it, my heart melts. As we began our second run, I called "come, heel," and she came to my left and looked up at me intensely.

Let's go!

Out of the corner of my eye, I saw movement. It was a squirrel, walking across the field, tantalizing. I steeled myself for Sheila to take off. I saw her nose quiver—she smelled the squirrel.

"Look at me," I said.

Sheila looked at me and I gave her a cookie. I saw her eyes shift left, then back to me. "Stay!" I said as I walked out ahead of her. As I turned my back, I expected her to take off, chasing after the squirrel, but when I turned to face her she was there, eyes pinned on me. A shiver went up my spine. I could see the squirrel swishing its tail. Sheila's eyes caught the movement. I saw it. I called, "Come *jump!*" and she ran to me, clearing the obstacle with at least six inches to spare. We ran to the second jump; she stayed with me as we took the dog walk, the weave poles, faced a complicated serpentine—jump out, come to me, back *out*—and there she was, face-to-face with the squirrel. There was a brief hesitation on her part while my heart leapt in my chest, but then she swung her body around toward me and took the last two jumps, running by my side. She was deliriously happy. She grabbed her cookies, tail wagging, excited. She was still off leash. The squirrel was still on the field. Sheila was basking in her success. Irina got out of her chair and walked toward me. Our eyes met.

"Did you *see* that?" I asked.

Irina smiled. "I did."

"She saw the 's-q.' I know she did."

"Of course she did. She chose to stay and play. That's powerful."

"I can't *believe* it."

"This was a dog that was supposed to die," Irina said. "Hah! Look at her now."

There she was: head held high, a slim, muscle-bound body, tail wagging. Sheila had defied the odds. She'd flourished even. She'd faced the demon squirrel and triumphed.

"Wasn't she supposed to lose enthusiasm for life?" Irina chuckled.

Agility did this, Irina was telling me in her funny way. *Agility made this dog strong; agility made this dog grow up and enjoy work. Agility put this dog back on her feet and helped her choose to stay on the field instead of chasing after silly old squirrels.*

I THINK AGILITY PUT BOTH Sheila and me back on our feet. It also created a strong connection between us—one that allowed Sheila to transcend her deeply rooted instincts. She chose to stay with me instead of chasing a squirrel. It was a shock to my system. If Sheila could ignore a squirrel in her path, well, *anything* was possible.

Things were looking up . . . or at least, they were changing.

I'd worked so hard, for so many years, and I'd finally seen a fantastic result. Sheila had broken my heart over and over—and she'd mended it with one miraculous choice. There were so few areas in my life where effort had translated to a surprisingly joyful payoff. It was a big moment for me.

The fixed stubbornness that Sheila had demonstrated throughout her life had budged. That was deeply moving and meaningful to me. We can also experience that same fixed and stubborn state in life. For some reason, we feel paralyzed and can't break free from bad habits, a negative state of mind, or even an emotional obsession. It seems like things will never change. But they can. They do.

I discovered this truth in my own life when Henry made one last appeal to resume our relationship. His rationale? We were older, wiser, and had both failed to fall in love with anyone else.

Like Sheila, I saw temptation in the distance. My glance flickered in his direction, but I kept my eyes forward. Damned if I wasn't going to run this course of mine and enjoy it. I'd worked too hard to give up now. The days of compulsion were over. I was done with fear, finished with hostile silence. I had work to do. I chose to stay on course.

I chose happiness.

Saved.

The last time I saw Henry I was driving through his neighborhood on the way home from agility. I saw his familiar walk and turned my head. I couldn't believe my eyes.

Henry was walking a dog.

I beeped the horn, smiled at him, and drove on.

HELLO, WORLD

I am generally a very private person. I like toiling in obscurity. It suits me. When I developed a nonfiction book project with a partner, however, the first comments from publishers were, "Where's your platform?"

Ah.

Blogs, Twitter, and Facebook were fast becoming de rigueur for writers, especially in the nonfiction arena. Social networking participation requires coming out of the shadows, jumping into the online conversation, and going public with your thoughts, opinions, and personality.

The project I'd developed with a partner was a good one; it had social value and it was needed. It was a simple format for friends to coach friends over lunch—sharing knowledge and experience—and it was a simple contribution to the economic and employment woes many people were experiencing.

To engage the world in this good idea, I needed to spread the word. Developing an online social platform is not an easy task. While I was skilled at advertising and marketing, this discipline was quite different; it's up-front and personal. There was no hiding, no way to present an idea separate from myself. I was the ambassador for this great and worthwhile concept. I had to learn to shake hands and kiss a few babies. Social networking is very much like an online cocktail party. It requires wit, charm, and engagement with all types of people from every walk of life. It also requires personal exposure. People want to know you and your core beliefs.

I'm rather personable at real cocktail parties, but this was different. I was basically talking to strangers. It was scary. I *dreaded* it.

But I did it. I launched a blog. I conversed in 140 characters. I supported other people who were developing worthwhile projects of their own, I developed a small fan base, and I posted on Facebook—I went public.

Wow.

What a wonderful world I discovered. Support, kindness, and generosity were rampant. I found like-minded friends in Australia, Europe, China, across the United States, and even in my own backyard. These online friends became even more real through video chats on Skype and offers of collaborative efforts and practical assistance.

It was a lesson—a big one. For years, I'd asked my dogs to perform all kinds of difficult tasks, and they'd willingly stepped outside their comfort zones for me.

Of course it was my turn.

* * *

DRIVE, SHE SAID

I don't know what got into Irina that day on the agility field. She was in a very good mood. Irina is rarely in a good mood. It was a delightful experience. She was lighthearted and silly. Goofy. Class was hilarious. The dogs joined in on the fun, happy for all the smiles and laughter. Of course, Nairobi thought he was responsible. Sheila was simply pleased to take part. She didn't care who was responsible.

After the dogs had finished their runs, Irina and I talked for a few minutes about agility. I made a comment about how different it must be to run a border collie instead of a ridgeback. She answered, "Try it."

"Huh?"

"You should run Rocket."

Rocket was an agility champion. He'd travelled the world with Irina and had won numerous championships. In the agility world, Rocket was a star. He was also all business. Border collies aren't motivated by food; they are in it for the work. A reward for a border collie after a run is a ball thrown that they can chase and bring back to you. *Cookies? Who needs those?*

But Rocket was not your average collie. Rewards were meaningless to him; he just wanted to run and jump and win—*everything*.

Rocket watches television. Believe me, he actually watches television. I've seen it. He likes the BBC news, nature documentaries, and any program on animals. Occasionally, he'll watch a science fiction movie if the visuals are interesting. If Irina turns to a channel he doesn't like, he gives her a long stare. When she switches to a program he likes, he turns to the TV screen with rapt attention. When the commercials come on, Rocket goes to get a drink of water and returns when the program resumes. Rocket also likes to watch his agility videos on the computer. He sits in Irina's chair at her desk and studies his videos. If you look at his face, you can see his eyes track his image on the screen. He often has a soft toy in his mouth as he watches himself perform, and he chews on it excitedly. When the video is over, he looks at Irina as if to say, "Play it again, please." Rocket will watch himself for hours at a time. It's like he's watching his game replay video, analyzing his performance. It's one of the strangest things I've ever seen.

Rocket has been at every agility class since I began training. He sits in a kennel in Irina's van and observes. If my dogs are doing well, he chews on his stuffed toy, urging the ridgebacks on. If the ridgebacks aren't doing well, he barks. *Jump right, not left! Come on! You can do it!*

The first time Irina and I took Sheila over the dog walk, Rocket watched with his crazy, focused eyes on Sheila the entire time. Rocket was *willing* her over that obstacle.

Needless to say, I was intimidated by Rocket. I suspected he was smarter than I was. He was certainly a lot faster.

"Okay. I'll do it," I said unconvincingly. "But you need to show me how to run him."

Irina patiently walked the course with me. Since Rocket would likely be ahead of me most of the course, it required a different kind of handling. I was used to getting my dogs to come and then run alongside them. With a dog like Rocket, it's all about the "send" command. There's no way I could run as fast as Rocket. My job was simply to direct him, but not just show him one jump ahead; I had to show him at least five jumps ahead. Running a border collie is like being an air traffic controller. You have to see the whole course, not one obstacle at a time.

I swallowed hard when Irina let Rocket onto the field. He's not an overly friendly dog; he's a working dog. Once he realized that I was going to take him for the run, he looked at me like I was his superior officer. *What's my assignment, Sergeant?*

As instructed, I placed him on the starting line. He looked up at me with a fierce expression. "Speak," I said.

Rocket barked.

"Speak."

He barked, staring at me with burning eyes.

"Speak."

He barked. *Get going!*

Wow.

"Stay," I said as I walked onto the field. Rocket crouched down, ready to fly.

I walked five jumps ahead and looked back at the black-and-white ball of ferocious energy, waiting for me to start the game.

Whoa.

"Come, *jump!*"

Rocket flew over the jumps and reached me in two seconds. I was late with the next sequence of jumps, but he did not slow down, and he took the next five jumps while I just pointed and called, "Jump, left! Go, jump! Right, jump!" I could barely get the words out.

This was like driving a Ferrari—an adrenaline rush. The power was overwhelming.

I was giddy.

Turned out, I liked a little speed.

"Okay, not bad," Irina called out, "but you have to go a lot faster sending him to the last line of jumps."

Right.

We went back to the starting line. It was a blur of barks and a whirling dervish of a dog and running and calling out commands.

Damn! My mind doesn't even work as fast as this dog!

One more run and we came close to good. Irina chuckled, which is a lot better that having her yell at me.

"That's an experience. *Incredible*," I gushed.

Irina put Rocket back into the car.

Class was over.

My mind was blown.

AS I DROVE HOME, RELIVING the Rocket-runs in my mind, it dawned on me that Irina had trusted me with her dog. Irina doesn't trust many people with her dogs; she won't even let her students pet her dogs. That was a milestone. I'd gained Irina's confidence. I wasn't sure how I'd done it, but I was happy to have it be so.

I also rededicated myself to the ridgeback pace. I liked speed, but I resonated more with my slow soul mates.

Ferraris are fun to drive—just not every day.

OUT OF AFRICA

"I never told you this, but these classes, this sport . . . it's become a spiritual and emotional formation for me," I began.

Irina looked down at the ground, listening.

"I take the lessons and what you teach me about the dogs, and I apply it to my life. I never told you this, but agility has had a huge effect on me. It's put me in touch with essential truths about myself. Just paying attention to the dogs, learning about their natures, training them . . . it's changed me."

Irina was quiet.

"I know agility has all been about the dogs, but really, as they've grown, I've grown. I'm a different person now."

Irina looked off into the distance. When she does that, she tilts her head; a very small smile appears on her face. At those moments, she reminds me of Sheila.

"You should write about it," Irina finally said.

OUT OF AFRICA HAS ALWAYS been one of my favorite books. I also loved the movie, with its sweeping vision of a precious land at a specific moment in history—the delicately drawn characters, each striving to find their place in the world. I admired Karen Blixen (Isak Dinesen) and her ability to write about her life adventure with such elegance, sense of place . . . and melancholy. The idea of a woman taking a journey to discover her soul is precious to me. I responded to this woman's courage and determination. She planted roots in foreign soil; she respected the unfamiliar and tried to understand it—and its effect on her. Somewhere in the process, she became an integral part of it, and it of her. The land and its people knew her and felt her presence.

I didn't take an exotic trip to find myself. The closest I ever got to Africa was owning two Rhodesian ridgebacks. Nevertheless, I took a journey. I travelled fifteen miles from my home and planted roots on a dusty field behind a sometime-Methodist, sometime-Korean Evangelical Church that also leased space to the local AA chapter and a belly dancing class. Nairobi was just a youngster when I took him to his first class. We had no idea that our lives were about to change. At least, I didn't. I can't speak for Nairobi.

I'd seen agility competitions on television and naively thought it looked like a fun sport. It seemed like a different way of training a dog than the authoritative "sit, stay because I say so" method.

I was one of the first Cesar Millan fans. I love the way he works with dogs, and I admire his authority with them—and his deep understanding of their nature. I understood the "pack leader" concept. It's profoundly clear. It works. But to be frank, I was on a different path. I had a bit of anarchy in my soul. I didn't really want to be anyone's leader. I wanted dogs—and the people around me—to choose to do the right thing. I also wanted to make the right choices in life—naturally. I had an undeveloped, but highly romantic, vision of a different kind of world—surrounded by a group of independent thinkers who came together in a like-minded spirit. In this world, people chose to be with me, they wanted to work with me. My dogs would work *with* me, not just obey me; they would want to do the things I asked—just like the man in my life would want to do nice things for me.

Well, on that dry patch of land behind the ecumenical/utopian dream of evangelical Christianity, AA, and belly dancing, I found just that. I found that spark in my animals—that desire to work with me and for me with pleasure. I stumbled onto the key to inspiring that desire . . . and once I felt that spirit of cooperation, willingness, and joyful spirit in my animals, it echoed inside. The moment I experienced it, I wanted more—I wanted it for myself.

I then turned around and looked at every single person in my life and began to ask for the same.

I lost a few people along the way. But I found a great deal more than I lost.

I found my Africa.

I tilled the soil. I got to know the locals. I planted seeds and waited for the crops to grow. There was romance and heartbreak. The rains came.

All while this was happening, I was growing—steady and strong. My dogs were by my side. It was never clear who was leading the way. We were following a scent.

In a mysterious way, we were leading one another.

It was harvest time.

Connections

chapter twelve

When your dog is on leash, connection is ensured.
Without it, staying close is up to the dog.

If you've built the right foundation with your dog,
the connection will remain.

Human connections are a different story.

I n agility, the handler brings the brains (hopefully) and the communication skills (sometimes), and the dog brings his athletic ability, his cooperation, and his willingness to engage in the game.

This game, however, is built on a very specific connection between the dog and the handler. I've watched many people run their dogs, and I'm always struck by either the presence—or the lack—of a strong connection. What I always see is the dog's connection to his handler. Inevitably, there is a look, a glance, a "what's next" communication from the dog, which the handler is sometimes oblivious to.

Dogs know that being close to people is a good thing. That's why they "dog" us. Whether it began 15,000 years ago when dogs scavenged for refuse at campsites of Paleolithic man, at some point in their long relationship with humans, dogs decided that being near us was an advantage.

The conventional wisdom is that the successful evolution and domestication of dogs has everything to do with their desire to please humans. I asked Irina her thoughts about this one day.

"I have a point of view that is not very popular in this regard," Irina began. "I don't believe dogs exist to please people. Actually, if a dog's behavior resembles a 'desire to please,' i.e. shows inferiority, subservience, or any action where the dog has to sacrifice his interests in my favor just to 'please' me, I go to great lengths to rid the dog of such notions. I happen to respect dogs and that 'I live to please you, Master' attitude just annoys me. I like to level with dogs, help them stand tall, make their own decisions, and take responsibility for their actions. In a nutshell, I like team play."

I respect Irina's point of view.

It's not that I don't believe dogs want to please; clearly, they do. I'm just more interested in a deeper—or higher—connection with my dogs. Dogs can make choices. We can control their behavior to a certain extent, and we can keep them on leash, but there will always be moments when a dog is off leash and faced with a choice. He can choose to listen to your voice or not. A dog trusts you or he doesn't. Like Sheila, who chose to ignore the squirrel on that amazing day at the agility field, all dogs can learn to discriminate between options—if we train them and invite them to do so.

Irina is remarkably connected to her dogs—a bit too close for my comfort, but I admire her for the respect she shows to her pack of three. Irina doesn't eat separately from her dogs; when she eats, they eat. She also shares her food with her dogs.

"But what if your dogs don't like what you're eating?" I asked.

"I don't eat anything that my dogs don't like. That's not fair."

Hmm.

Lest you think Irina is dog-crazed, she is not. She's often spoken of a future for herself without dogs. She is neither sentimental nor overly romantic about dogs; she simply treats them with extraordinary dignity.

THE CONNECTION DOGS HAVE TO their humans is resolute. It's so seemingly effortless, this attachment dogs form with us, it's easy to dismiss. Their love is unconditional, and their greetings are a joyful welcome after time apart. We suck up their unconditional love like soothing hot chocolate on a cold day.

But sometimes, at least in my house, it feels like there's a bit too much connecting going on. If I let them, the dogs would go everywhere with me—including the shower. I adore my dogs, but their constant need to stick close can drive me a little crazy. Every individual has a certain tolerance level for physical connection, and I reach my limit at some point every day, especially when Nairobi tries to "herd" me to the kitchen when he thinks it is dinnertime.

I am not a sheep.

If I don't want the dogs to follow me, I send them to "place," which is where they lie down. In my living room, their place is under my desk where their beds are side-by-side. Once in place, they are expected to stay until I release them. While this seems terrifically organized and sensible of me, it doesn't work without a great deal of effort. To avoid having the dogs underfoot while I'm making their dinner, I send them to "place," but inevitably, one or the other of them will try to sneak into the kitchen and get a jump on the dinner action. Usually, it's Nairobi, who creeps toward the smells wafting from the kitchen. "Nairobi!" I say loudly. "Go to place!"

He scampers back to place and pretends to lie down; his behind is always several inches above the bed. "Down," I say. He stares at me, ears projecting like sails catching a strong wind.

"Down."

His butt goes a bit lower.

"Down."

Finally, he lays down.

I know I'm not supposed to repeat the command. I can't help myself.

Nairobi and Sheila both wait until I call "come," and then there is a mad dash for the kitchen. Here again, I try to set up some boundaries so that I don't get overrun by charging ridgebacks.

"Come front."

They both sit in front of me and wait until I've placed their dinner bowls on the floor. I then say, "Look at me." They stare at me with such intensity that I have to hold back my laughter. Nairobi drools, copiously. We all look at one another for at least thirty seconds until I say okay, and they lunge at their food bowls and gobble it all up.

I consider the boundaries I've set up as a form of organized connection. And I have to set clear ones, otherwise my dogs will knock me down in pursuit of their goals.

IN MY LIFE, CONNECTIONS WITH people have felt transitory—even ephemeral. I have done my share of disconnecting, especially with Henry, but it's an odd, sometimes brutal, thing we humans do. I can't imagine a dog saying, "I've had enough of you! I'm leaving!" I also can't imagine a dog forgetting his family. Dogs that have been separated from their mothers and siblings for years always recognize one another if they are brought into contact. They can even smell their family if they are in proximity. Dogs separated from their owners also recognize them years later. Dogs can find their way home from hundreds of miles away.

Dogs don't forget.

People leave and forget one another all the time. We discard one another like old clothes.

Dogs seem to know that we have this tendency to wander away, which may be why dogs stay so close to their humans.

Of course, sometimes leaving is a good thing, a smart thing, even the right thing. We get a choice about whom we connect with, and when that connection has come to an end, others follow.

* * *

BEAUTIFUL DOGS

My dogs think that outside of our house, they have another name: Beautiful Dogs. It's the phrase they hear most when I take them on walks in my neighborhood. Passersby, shop owners, kids, folks in passing cars, and even tough-looking street types comment, "*Beautiful* dogs . . ." Each time Nairobi and Sheila hear those words, they turn to the speaker calmly, in unison, as if to say, "Yes. That's us."

For those few people who actually recognize the breed, the words become "*Beautiful* ridgebacks," and sometimes it's shortened to just an excited: "Ridgebacks!"

But as every ridgeback breeder or owner will tell you, ridgebacks are not for everyone, especially first-time dog owners. Anyone who's ever owned a hound can testify to the fact that they are tough to train, and ridgebacks can be even more challenging. They can act like overgrown lap dogs, and hardly seem to understand that eighty pounds of weight is an issue for the human being they're crushing beneath their sleeping bodies They are the nap-in-the-sun, curl-up-on-the-couch kind of animals and can wait days, even weeks, for a little excitement. But when the action appears, a ridgeback will spring to life, taking off in pursuit of prey with muscle-bound finesse and a deep, throaty bark.

When a ridgeback runs toward you, take a defensive position.

I first fell in love with the breed at a local Little League game. One of the parents brought the family pet, a gorgeous ridgeback named Kenya. I'd never seen a dog with so much personal presence and dignity. She sat serenely on the bleachers and watched the game as if she knew exactly what was going on. The youngest child in the family had her arm thrown around Kenya, and when the girl got excited, she'd pull the dog close to her in a tight hug. Kenya squinted a bit, but was otherwise stoic.

Our Labrador, Samantha, had died several months before, and my boys and I were longing for a new dog. I had an instinct about Rhodesian ridgebacks, so I did some research. The more I read about the breed, the more convinced I was that this was the dog for us. Until then, every dog I'd had in my life chose me through circumstance or chance. This was the first time I chose the dog. Within a few weeks, I found a breeder in Orange County, and after an extensive phone interview, my oldest son and I visited her. *Oh, the puppies!* Baby ridgebacks are almost hairless and they have snubbed noses and deep frowns. They look like baby pigs. I loved them all. My son and I spent time with each one, but our attention was repeatedly drawn to a serious little fellow wearing a blue collar. He was sweet, gentle, and he kept looking at us with a thoughtful expression. He didn't rush to my son or squirm or even make much of a fuss like the other puppies. He looked self-contained. My son wouldn't let go of him, so the choice was made. We drove home that day with a six-week-old, fat puppy who had a steady, warm gaze. We liked his blue collar, so we named him Blue.

I formed an immediate, deep attachment to this special dog—and so did my boys. One of our funnier family stories, which my sons like to embarrass me with, is the day that Blue fell into the swimming pool. I had just come home from work, dressed in a skirt and heels, and I was walking the boys to the pool for a swim. Puppy Blue, just a few months old, followed happily behind us. When the boys jumped into the pool, so did Blue. With no exposure to water yet, he just sank to the bottom. Without thinking, I jumped in after him, high heels first, and plummeted straight to the bottom of the pool. I grabbed Blue and swam to the surface. It happened so fast, none of us had time to react, but then the boys burst into hysterical laughter at the sight of their fully dressed mother, treading water while holding aloft a drenched puppy.

Blue grew into a tall, sweet-tempered, lanky companion. He was wise, gentle, and soulful, and he smiled when he was embarrassed, drawing his lips back to show a sheepish grin. I learned quickly not to raise my voice with him—the hurt look in his eyes, curled-under tail, and lowered head revealed how sensitive he was. All Blue needed was a soft *uh-uh* and he'd stop any undesirable behavior. He was an endearing, one-of-a-kind dog that licked tears softly from my face and nestled protectively with my kids when they were frightened or sad.

Blue liked other dogs, but never socialized with them. When we'd go to the dog park, Blue would run a few steps toward the excited pack, lift his head as if to say "Hi!" and then he'd return to my side. He seemed to think his job was to stay near, sitting tightly next to me, leaning against my leg.

Blue had a special relationship with my boys, especially my youngest son who was living in the shadow of a dominant older brother. At six, my youngest was trying to compete with a ten-year-old, which was frustrating, if not futile, for him. Blue seemed to understand this. I would often find Blue curled up beside my son on the floor as he watched TV or played video games. He would often talk to Blue, telling him stories, explaining the TV show or the intricacies of certain video game strategies. Blue listened.

When we lost Blue to lymphoma at just four years old, it was a severe blow to all of us. He had been diagnosed six months before, and while I knew he wasn't going to live long, my young sons had fantasies of a miracle. Blue's death was crushing. We cried for months. We knew we could never replace him, but we also knew when it was time, we would get another ridgeback.

When we were ready to risk our hearts again with another dog, I found a breeder with a litter and got our second ridgeback. We named him Nairobi Blues. I once met a doctor from Nairobi who told me that Nairobi meant "the rains have come." In the dry climate of Africa, rains bring pleasure and promise, so we chose the name Nairobi. "Blues" was in honor of Blue.

From the start, Nairobi was an unusual puppy. He was quite focused on us and wanted to be in someone's lap or arms all the time. I was bowled over by the intensity of emotion this little, short-haired, brown-eyed boy elicited from me. His favorite position was on my chest with his front paws wrapped tightly around my neck. He hugged hard. When I'd try to disentangle myself, he'd let out a low growl, as if to say, *Stay with me, don't move, let's just cuddle!* I'd never experienced a dog with such a deep need for a physical connection, and when I'd catch him staring at me from across the room with a soulful look, I could feel the emotion flooding from him.

Nairobi still looks at me that way.

Raising and training a dog means you're needed from the moment you hold that warm puppy in your arms until he takes his last breath. And all along the journey of a dog's lifetime, he never stops needing your guidance, love, and instruction.

And lucky us that we get to experience the entire life span of our dogs, and learn again and again through the lives of many dogs, the simple yet profound lessons they have to teach us.

All we have to do is listen.

DOG WALKING

Daily walks provide the perfect opportunity to demonstrate positive connections. Every good walk builds a bridge between me and my dogs.

Our day starts slowly. Since I'm a night owl, we don't hit the road for our walk until ten or eleven in the morning. While I drink my coffee, the dogs wait for me either sunning on the porch or curled up at the bottom of my bed. The ridgebacks like a leisurely approach to the day. Thank goodness for that.

We walk together every day. I have four or five walking routes to choose from and I try to vary them so the dogs don't get bored. My theory about dog walking is a mixture of things I've learned from Irina and a few of my own ideas. The dogs do their business within the first five minutes of the walk. They usually eliminate in the same place, at the same time. This was fairly easy to teach with treats and praise when they were younger, and they've kept it up. After that, we walk at a fast pace and always do some small training along the way. I consider my dogs my companions, and I don't ignore them when we're walking together. By connecting to my dogs on our walks, I'm showing them respect. They return the favor.

Of course, while I think I'm doing the walking, my dogs believe that they are in charge of getting me away from work and out into the fresh air. In a way, they're right. It's the dogs that are doing the discovery as we walk; they see people and animals and birds and pick up new scents. Every walk is a brand new experience. I follow their lead as much as they follow mine.

That said, I don't want to give the impression that our walks are all peace and light. Our first issues begin before we've left the house. As I get ready, the dogs are circling around me. They circle slowly, as ridgebacks do, but still, I can't move for the all muscle-bound bulk of them. When they stop moving, (usually, after I yell, "Stop!") Nairobi lies between the bathroom and the bedroom so I have to step over him to go anywhere, and Sheila stands next to the closet so I can't get into it.

The ridgebacks are like sentries, guarding every direction I might conceivably take. They have every exit covered.

"Ridgebacks, go *away*."

That sends them out of my room to stand in the hallway.

"Sit."

They comply and I continue to get ready, but those clever dogs, as soon as my back is turned, one or the other of them comes back into my room and tries to trip me.

After I'm finally ready, it's the "race to the door." This is Sheila's specialty. She wants to be the first through the door and will shove me aside like a school yard bully to get out of the house before me. This necessitates more organization.

"Ridgebacks, *sit*. Now, *wait*."

I open the door, step through, and then they are allowed out of the house. Nairobi is thrilled, jumping and twirling in excitement as if this has never happened before. *Could we be going for a walk?!* As soon as I've shut the door, I wonder, *Did I lock the front door?* I reenter the house and Nairobi races by my side. *Is it locked? Can we go now?* Once I'm satisfied that the door is secured, Nairobi tries to herd me to the back door, looking up at me, prancing, jumping; he can hardly contain himself. He leaps out of the back entrance, tackling Sheila with exuberance. They growl and roughhouse until I call, "Ridgebacks! Come, front." Both dogs sit while I put on their collars and leashes. The same *me first* routine plays out as we leave out of the back gate. Again, Sheila is obsessed with getting through the gate before Nairobi or me. For some strange reason, I have never been able to train the ridgebacks fully with regard to the door issue. Every day, it's as if it was the first time they ever heard of the "Carol goes first" rule. They always seem so surprised.

And for some strange reason, I can never remember whether I've locked the front door or not.

Everything with the dogs, however, goes more smoothly with a cookie in my pocket. My forgetfulness remains unsolved.

Once we hit the road, the peculiarities continue. Nairobi knows very well what "heel" means. He's quite capable of it. Yet, his enthusiasm goads him, and he trots ahead. Before I know it, he's a good foot ahead of Sheila and me.

"Nairobi, heel."

He glances over his shoulder—*Oh! Sorry!*—and slows down a bit and resumes position, but five minutes later, he's at it again, out front, oblivious. *Let's go! What's that? Who's that? Let's go!*

Nairobi's curiosity moves his body. *Is there a dog in that car?* He will veer wildly to check, head up, nose in the air, ears akimbo. When Nairobi leans, there is eight pounds of muscle behind him, and if he gets some traction, God help me.

Sheila is very good walking on either my left or my right. Her issue is closeness; she likes to give me a wide berth, but will then veer in toward me when she's alarmed by something.

When one big dog is slightly ahead—the other to your side—and they both decide to move into your path, get ready to say hello to the pavement.

My preemptive strike is training. With cookies in my hands, I can get my dogs' attention and we manage quite well. The other trick I use when the ridgebacks are daydreaming is suddenly calling out, "Turn left!" and we make a complete circle to the left. This always gets them to pay attention. "Turn right!" and off we go, circling to the right.

What's she going to do now? Why are we going in circles? Do we get cookies for this?

Yes. I have many tricks up my sleeve.

There is no antidote to my mind-wanderings, though. When I get distracted by my thoughts, trouble usually follows.

Leaning down to clean up after my dogs one day, I was thinking of something else, and suddenly the dogs lunged at a small barking dog passing by. Both leashes slipped out of my hand. No one likes to see two massive dogs running toward their little dog, and the woman quickly picked up her dog. I grabbed mine and apologized profusely.

Grr.

Mindfulness is all.

It's a struggle for me.

BIG DOGS, SMALL SPACES, AND WARM BLANKETS

Once the work day starts and I am in front of my computer, the dogs sleep under my desk in their beds. It's a very pleasant way to work. Both dogs go outside to sit in the sun and return to me—and generally they sleep all day.

After dinner, the dogs are allowed to cuddle up on the bottom of my bed. I lay out a clean chenille blanket that I wash daily. The dogs know that the blankets get washed every day. Sheila often stands in front of the washer after the cycle has finished, reminding me that it's time to put the laundry in the dryer. After twenty minutes, Sheila jockeys into position as I open the dryer door. With her tail wagging mightily, she sticks her nose in, excited. *Warm blankets! Yay!* She races to my room, and as I lay out the blanket, she's the first to jump up and quickly curls into a ball. Nairobi follows suit, but instead of snuggling beside Sheila, he lies on top her; she is his pillow, his heating pad, his hot spot. I then put a second chenille blanket over them, covering them entirely. They generate so much heat in this configuration under the blanket they could probably heat a small house. Ridgebacks like warmth. They are short-haired dogs.

Happy to oblige.

While they are ensconced at the bottom of my bed, I sit down to write. A half hour into my work, Nairobi creeps out of the bedroom and stands next to me, whining. Sometimes the blanket is still draped over him and he looks like ridgeback royalty. What does he want? He wants me to go back into the bedroom and rearrange the blanket for him. Either Sheila got up to stretch or he did. He now wants me to go and make it perfect for him.

I once told Irina this story and she said, "Teach Nairobi how to cover himself with the blanket. Rocket can do it."

Well, of course Rocket can do it.

Needless to say, I have not taught Nairobi how to rearrange his blanket. That's what I'm here for.

The lovely thing about the blanket drama is that I am forced to leave my desk every half hour. While I rearrange the ridgebacks' sleeping arrangements, I am walking, bending, and taking a moment to stretch.

Thank you, Nairobi.

At midnight or 1:00 AM, I start to get ready for bed. The dogs are woozy with sleep. As soon as I begin to brush my teeth, Sheila, ever trying to be the best (or first) at everything, gets off the bed and heads for the kennels in the back room. Sheila always goes to the kennel nearest the window. It's the same routine every night. Nairobi is unconscious on my bed, waiting until the last minute before stirring. I finish my nightly rituals and call, "Nairobi, go kennel." He always looks at me in disbelief. It takes him several minutes to digest the horrible news. He's also waiting for a possible reprieve. *Maybe I will let him sleep in my bed?* It will never happen. Nairobi is a restless sleeper and spreads out, covering the entire width and length of the bed. I defy anyone to try to sleep with Nairobi.

Finally, Nairobi faces the fact that he must go to his kennel. He arises slowly, jumps off the bed, and gives a long ridgeback stretch. He then looks over his shoulder at me. *You coming?* I dutifully follow him into the back room, and he walks to Sheila's kennel where she lies, waiting for him. He stands at her kennel door, looking at her. Sometimes he bangs the kennel door with his paw and makes it swing wildly. Nairobi wants to sleep in the kennel Sheila has chosen. I don't know if Nairobi really prefers this kennel, likes messing with Sheila, or simply wants to get into a kennel that has been warmed already. Whatever the reason, it's the same routine every night. I usher Nairobi into the other kennel and he collapses, done for the night.

I KNOW I COULD TRAIN ALL these eccentricities out of my dogs. I could train them to use specific kennels, I could work harder on the "who goes first" door issue, and I could have more control on walks if I took them out separately. I understand all this.

I have deliberately left some problems unsolved.

Why?

I like it when Robi jumps up to give me a kiss. Call me perverse, but I also like it when he jumps up on visitors. It helps me see who they are.

Sorry, everyone.

Perhaps we've forgotten, but dogs are not furry people, they are animals. Sure, we should train them to fit in with civilized life—to a certain degree. The rest? It's golden. The imperfections, the flaws— they are precious to me. They both infuriate and amuse me. They also remind me of my own unfinished self. There is a part of dog behavior that I just like to watch. It reminds me of the truth about life, and each time I see their oddness, I feel a bit better about my own.

Perfection—the desire for perfect children, bodies, relationships, and careers—is a huge, sad phenomenon in our society. There will always be someone who can run faster, sell more, or beat you at your own game. The sense of a "perfect time" is also a terrible burden. We rush to hit our life stages and achieve our goals as if we were running out of time. "Do it *now* or the opportunity will be lost forever!"

Wait just a minute. Who set this schedule?

A friend of mine began studying for her Masters degree in her late thirties and her younger brother's response was, "Why bother? Isn't it too late?"

What a horrible thing to say.

Until there is no time, there is ample time—to find one's self, to learn, to expand your world. It doesn't matter if you're five years old or eighty-five; personal revelation doesn't have an expiration date. Throughout a lifetime, there is always a chance to reverse direction, to try something new.

Contrary to the well-known saying, old dogs *can* learn new tricks.

Just ask Nairobi.

Given that both dogs and humans move at their individual paces, it just makes sense to allow the unfinished, the half-done, the almost-there—even the half-baked. You never know where someone is in the process of becoming. Accepting, even enjoying, one another's flaws is both a reminder to keep forging ahead on your own life adventure, and also, to let it be.

I WAS AT MY BOOK club meeting—five women's excuse for getting together to drink wine, eat good food, and talk—and we began discussing books we'd loved as children. Serendipitously, we all had the same favorite author, Noel Streatfeild.

The most famous of her books is *Ballet Shoes,* but the author went on to write a series of books about capable, rational children succeeding in the adult world. Ms. Streatfeild's books were about children developing careers, and as a young girl, I loved the idea of a child working, even saving her family. The lesson learned from these books was that while talent was important, hard work and following the rules led to success. I also got the very clear impression from the author that children were inherently wise—a very heartening message for a child.

I was so devoted to Noel Streatfeild as a child, I wrote her a letter.

> *Dear Miss Streatfeild,*
> *I love your books. I want to be a writer just like you when*
> *I grow up and work with animals, too.*
> *Love,*
> *Carol*

During that book club meeting, I remembered the letter. It also dawned on me that my deep appreciation of the "child as a hero" theme that Noel Streatfeild so elegantly illustrated was very close to my feelings about the "dog as a hero" theme that resonated with me. The relative innocence and simplicity of children pitted against the complex, agenda-ridden adult world fit closely with my vision of where dogs fit into our world. These heroic children in literature navigate the thorny, complicated adult world—and the children's good sense and purpose wins out. It's the same with dogs who lack the guile to compete with humans, and yet, they get their way more often than not.

It was a moment of illumination, evidence of a bridge between the adult me and my eight-year-old self. I had the distinct feeling that I'd suddenly arrived home after a long journey. That memory of myself as a child rushed in.

Oh, hello! Nice to see you again!

All through this life of mine, there had been a theme; I'd simply forgotten it. I was, and am, the same soul—a longing, dreaming, imagining, and admiring girl, now disguised as a woman. The recognition was overwhelming, soothing. I was surrounded by the warm blanket of connection between the past and present, between who I'd wanted to be and who I became.

It was just a delicate thread—a not so original, but deeply precious idea formed in the mind of a child. What a lovely surprise to find that it had held fast.

ENDINGS

The finality of an ending is inescapable, but I've rarely been surprised by it. Usually, I can see it coming. Often, I've been the initiator. Not this time.

The field where I'd had class with Irina for so many years was in the process of being sold. Irina reorganized her classes and announced that she'd given my regular time slot to someone else. My heart skipped a beat when she told me. It was a weird feeling. She offered me another time, but my schedule didn't allow it.

Whoa.

I couldn't quite absorb the details. It happened too quickly. She me sent a text. I sent her back an email. And that was that.

Emails—first with Henry, now Irina. Doesn't anyone break up in person anymore?

Before I knew it, in one swift digital exchange, my agility classes with Irina were over.

I COULD HAVE PICKED UP the phone and begged for my class time back. It might have worked, but I couldn't bring myself to insist on being with anyone who wasn't enthusiastic about being with me. Our connection had simply run its course.

Leaving when your time is up is an art. I've stayed too long and I've left too early; this time, it felt just right.

So, I moved on.

It was painful for about twenty-four hours. Then I felt a huge relief.

I was *thrilled!*

Overjoyed!

I felt like *dancing!*

My very long apprenticeship with my very tough master was over.

Good job, Carol!

I felt like I'd earned a medal. I'd graduated. I was now free to experience something entirely different.

Irina was an excellent teacher for me, the perfect teacher. I needed to come up against a strong personality in order to find out exactly what I was made of. I'm not sure I would have discovered so much about myself without the pressure she put me under. It was also Irina's teaching that inspired me to write this book. Her views on dogs and people motivated me to tell this story. Irina is a very wise and extremely intelligent woman—a formidable combination.

And her wisdom? Always to the point:

"Don't like dogs barking? Get a cat."

TELLING THIS STORY, I'VE THOUGHT a lot about Henry. I had no sense of timing where he was concerned. We did love one another. It just wasn't the kind of love meant for a lifelong partnership. We weren't made of the same stuff. We didn't possess the skills or tools to build a life together.

Our relationship should have begun and ended the first moment we met. A smile was shared, a soul connection made, acknowledged. That should have been the end of it.

I didn't know who I was then. On the surface, I was a successful woman with two great kids, two great dogs, and one loving fiancé. It was a pretty picture. It just wasn't my picture. That's hardly a good excuse for prolonging our doomed love affair for as long as I did, but it's the only one I have. If I'd known myself, accepted and loved my own nature, I would never have stayed so long.

When I first met Henry, I was struggling to make my peace with living in difficulty because I knew it so well, but secretly, I wanted something different. I wanted happiness, even though I didn't really understand how to get it or even what it was. But it was in the back of my mind. It was in my heart.

Ending our relationship was right for me, though it was never a cause for celebration. It's hard to abandon the familiar, to let a loved one go. My heart goes out to every man and woman who has walked away from the wrong thing without a clear picture of where to go next.

My advice?

Get a dog.

BE HAPPY

I don't know the exact day that I decided I deserved happiness. Bells didn't ring, the clouds did not part. I simply said the words aloud and realized they were true.

Just because you choose happiness, a result doesn't necessarily come to you in a nicely wrapped package. You heart's desire isn't always sitting across from you on the bus or beside you on your flight to destinations unknown. It might not be heralded by a new job, new friends, or a new romance.

When I first got the idea for this book, an editor read the initial pages and asked about the end of the story. Was there a "happy" ending? I suspected that what she really meant was, "Did I lose the bad fiancé and find true love?"

While I wish I could provide such a neat ending, the journey I have taken has less to do with finding a man than finding myself.

I believe finding and learning to trust yourself is dramatic. The moment I learned the hard lessons I desperately needed to learn, my life changed in profound ways. I have confidence enough to stand in the sun and share what I've learned. Friends now turn to me for advice and counsel, they lean on me, and they trust my knowledge and experience because I did the hard work of turning my own life around. Completion of self does not mean finding a man; it means something much greater.

Now that I've learned to trust myself, my thoughts about love have changed. The types of men I'd chosen in the past—Henry and all the Henry-like men I've ever known—are ghosts. They haunt me. Having a relationship with a different kind of man, learning how to be in a relationship that doesn't involve control and my passive resistance to that control, is a new experience. Listening to a man's words without interpreting them in my mind, and judging a man by his actions not his intentions—these things are coming more easily now. All my preconceived notions about intellect, sophistication, degrees, age, and careers have been tossed aside. Good men come in strange packages sometimes. I suppose good women do, too. Dogs *definitely* do.

Happiness, though, lives quite contentedly apart from a romantic ending to a story.

And happiness is not a *thing*.

I think this is why I've had such a difficult time wrestling with the concept of happiness all these years. It seemed like a result. A destination. An object.

Granted, I have a literal mind. I think in concrete terms. But happiness isn't a tangible reality outside of one's existence; it's the way you take the experiences of life into yourself. You can take a breath without giving it a thought—or you can note each wondrous one.

I THINK THERE ARE MANY people who have a tentative connection with life. Maybe we got a bit bruised at the beginning or somewhere along the way. We were never convinced of the wonderful promises that were shared, the fantastic stories that were told. We saw those Hollywood movies and appreciated them, but at the same time, we were alienated by the sense that our lives were not tied up with such clear plot points. Everyone in our lives misbehaved, ourselves included. We were less than heroes. We found ourselves reacting instead of acting. Life seemed scary. Surprising. Weird. Painful. Really awkward at times. Strangers in a strange land, we iffy souls have a challenge: How to live?

I came to realize that the answer to that question was neither elusive nor divorced from my personal experience.

Wisdom isn't out there, it's here.

Faith isn't an idea, it's what you do.

My dogs taught me this.

To me, it doesn't matter what route anyone takes to wholeness and compassion. Concepts or religions or people speak to us at certain points in our lives. Relationships can change everything. Love and children and wise elders can make all the difference.

But for me, it was dog wisdom that moved my heart. Simple, sometimes painful lessons: take it step-by-step, work hard, train, live, enjoy. Follow the rules, be consistent, give rewards. Practice gratitude, kindness, love, and loyalty. Run fast, play hard, and kiss when you feel like it. Lean on the people close to you; be a part of a pack.

Don't be afraid of belonging.

I'M STAYING AT A FRIEND'S HOUSE on the beach and the dogs and I have just returned from a long walk. It is a cold day, and the ridgebacks ran crazily, kicking up sprays of sand, while the ocean roared, threatening to catch them up in the waves. But they are both suspicious of the ocean, so they kept their distance.

Every time I take my dogs to the beach, they avoid looking at the water. Instead, they lift their heads to stare out at the horizon past the long stretch of white sand. Their gaze seems to transport them back in time. I whisper dramatically, *"Ridgebacks!* It's *Africa!"* They wag their tails.

Now, inside the house, a fire crackling in the fireplace I have the distinct impression that I'm exactly where I should be. I have absolutely no wish to be anywhere else than where I am right now.

Sheila hears the strange popping sounds from the fireplace and comes to my side. Her head rests on my knee, trembling.

Nairobi scratches his back against the couch with his eyes on us. *What's up guys? What's the trouble? Isn't it time for dinner?*

How did we get here—to this perfect moment? Evocative of all that came before, yet remarkably attuned to the promise of adventures to come.

Yes.

It's time.

Resources and Links

DOG AGILITY

There are three main agility associations in the United States. They are the United States Dog Agility Association (USDAA), the American Kennel Club (AKC), and the North American Dog Agility Council (NADAC). Each organization has its own set of rules and requirements. The USDAA has graciously allowed the following reprint from their website:

What dog is best suited for agility?

Any dog with good physical agility and energy is a strong candidate for the sport. Though many breeds appear more naturally adapted to the sport, more than 150 breeds (including mixed-breeds as a single group) have demonstrated their ability to perform well.

What is USDAA's philosophy on dog agility?

USDAA promotes dog agility as an athletic, spectator sport in its own right, as it offers enthusiasts a variety of competitive classes in addition to the standard agility class, such as gambler's choice where handlers choose the obstacles to be performed, team relay where handlers team up to run a course, jumpers where competitors demonstrate their training and handling expertise with their dogs performing a fast course comprised of various styles of jumps and hurdles, and snooker agility where handlers choose their route on course following the principal strategy rules of the billiards game of snooker.

Though agility is a competitive, athletic sport, USDAA also promotes dog agility as a community sport, as it offers families a fun alternative for spending quality time with their pet, whether in the Championship, Performance, or Junior Handler program. The obstacles are relatively easy to train, and a handler and their dog can do reasonably well and have fun without the hours of training required in other competitive canine activities; however, as with any sport, considerable time and energy is required to be highly competitive. As a commitment to promoting dog agility in the community, USDAA has developed a junior handler program for school-age children and their pets to encourage their participation and to teach responsible pet ownership.

What kind of events does USDAA have?

USDAA and its growing number of licensed groups across North America host agility certification classes to test a competitor's expertise in training and handling such that they fully demonstrate a dog's natural agility pursuant to standards established by USDAA's board of directors. Participants may earn certification titles, such as Agility Dog®, Advanced Agility Dog®, and Master Agility Dog® in USDAA's Championship Program, as well as titles offered through the USDAA Junior Handler Program and Performance Program. Certification titles are offered for both standard and nonstandard classes—standard agility, gambler's choice, snooker agility, jumpers and relay – to provide recognition for a wide variety of accomplishments. For those who excel, competitors may earn the coveted Agility Dog Champion® title, and continue to measure their excellence through bronze, silver, gold and platinum level designations in each class. Similar titles are offered in USDAA's Performance Program.

USDAA's competitive tournament events include the prestigious Grand Prix of Dog Agility® World Championships, Dog Agility Steeplechase®, and Dog Agility Masters® International Three-Dog Team Championship. Since the Grand Prix's inception in 1988, the tournament has grown to include more than 150 qualifying events each year that are held across the United States, Canada, Mexico, Puerto Rico, Bermuda, and Japan. The local qualifying events lead to regional championships and the World Championships. The Dog Agility Masters® team championships is a pentathlon event, which is promoted internationally, and the Dog Agility Steeplechase® championship features speed in jumping competition and carrying cash prizes up to more than $25,000 each year. Championships for all three tournaments are held as signature events at USDAA's Cynosport® World Games each fall.

You can find more information about dog agility at the following websites:

www.usdaa.com

www.akc.org/events/agility

www.nadac.com

For a general description of the history of agility, Wikipedia offers a great deal of information and a list of sources and books:

http://en.wikipedia.org/wiki/Dog_agility

To find an agility training school, a trainer, or a club in your area, you can contact the USDAA, the AKC, or the NADAC through their websites.

Agility is an international sport, and actually made its debut in England in the 1970s at the famed Crufts Dog Show. For information about the sport internationally, google the International Federation of Cynological Sports.

And if you have some free time, search on YouTube for dog agility videos. There are some wonderful videos online—as well as some very funny ones.

RHODESIAN RIDGEBACKS

To learn more about the breed, visit the Rhodesian Ridgeback Club of the United States: **www.rrcus.org**

LURE COURSING

Another fun sport to do with your dog—hounds only—is lure coursing. If you have a sight hound, this may be the sport for you. Visit:

www.asfa.org

www.akc.org/events/lure_coursing

ALL ABOUT DOGS

DOG AWARE is a comprehensive website on dog foods, including information and links on many specific health issues: **http:// dogaware.com**

B-NATURALS is a website for holistic supplements for dogs and cats. The site also contains many articles of interest for those who have specific heath issues or the desire to know more about canine nutrition: **www.b-naturals.com**

AHVMA.ORG is the official website of the American Holistic Veterinary Medical Association. Check this site for a list of holistic veterinarians in your area: **http://ahvma.org**

THE MERCK VETERINARY MANUAL is an online resource for animal care: **www.merckvetmanual.com**

THE HOLISTIC VET: Dr. Marc Bittan can be reached at **www.theholisticvet.com**

RESCUE ORGANIZATIONS

For information about adopting or fostering a dog or cat, go to: **www.petfinder.com**

BEST FRIENDS ANIMAL SOCIETY is a great adoption and rescue organization: **www.bestfriends.org**

DOGS DESERVE BETTER is a great rescue organization: **http://dogs-deservebetter.org**

SUPPORT

Sponsor a pet via Twitter: **www.adoptapet.com/twitteracritter**

PETS OF THE HOMELESS provides pet food and veterinary care to the homeless and less fortunate in local communities across the United States and Canada: **www.petsofthehomeless.org/**

Make a difference in the wake of natural disasters that leave dogs homeless, lost, or injured. Lend support to organizations like NOAH'S WISH, THE DISASTER RELIEF FUND OF THE HUMANE SOCIETY OF THE UNITED STATES, and the AMERICAN VETERINARY MEDICAL FOUNDATION.

IMPAIRED OR AGING DOGS

For information about senior pets: **http://aarff.com**

If you're living with a visually or hearing impaired dog or a dog with a disability, here are some great resources:

http://blinddogs.com

http://deafdogs.org

http://handicappedpets.com

http://petswithdisabilities.org

LOST DOGS

http://petharbor.com

www.fidofinder.com

GENERAL DOG RESOURCES

Information about dog-friendly hotels and travelling with your pets:

http://dogfriendly.com

Great information about dogs: **www.dogster.com**

Pet-friendly travel experts: **www.bringfido.com**

Here's a mobile **DOG PARK FINDER** app for the dog lover on-the-go:

http://itunes.apple.com/us/app/dog-park-finder-plus/id372419 544?mt=8

Here's a new website with the mission "To create dog equality and pro-mote responsible dog ownership:" **http://joinprojectdog.com**

The best overall site for all things dog is **http://thebark.com**, and *Bark Magazine* is wonderful. Dog Is My Co-Pilot® is the registered, trademarked motto of *Bark Magazine*. An anthology of some of the magazine's best stories was turned into a book: *Dog Is My Co-Pilot: Great Writers on the World's Oldest Friendship.*

Acknowledgments

A warm thank you to my agent, Al Zuckerman, whose support, guidance, and friendship has meant so much to me.

Much gratitude to Seal Press for delivering the wonderful editor, Merrik Bush-Pirkle—and also to Brooke Warner, who began this project. Appreciation to the entire Seal Press team for their hard work: Eva Zimmerman, my publicist; and designer Domini Dragoone, for her beautiful and sensitive cover art and interior design.

Many, many thanks to Andrea Raab Sherman, for her kindness, friendship, support, and for the extraordinary patience it took to read endless drafts—and trim my wandering prose.

To my friend and photographer, Rich Marchewka, thank you for catching all the right moments.

Thank you to my neighborhood pack: Eric, Michael, Pam, Mary, Susan, Mei, Andrew—and to the newest pack members, Miles and Theo.

To all my dogs: Winnie, Malcolm, Cana, Samantha, Zoe, Blue, Nairobi, and Sheila.

To my friends in social media who have been so gracious and helpful online—and off: @iggypintado, @HennArtOnline, @iconic88, @windowsot, @MomsOfAmerica, @jeffrago, @Beth-Frysztak, @teeco71, @Buttercupd, @mayhemstudios, @earthXplorer, @JoeTheProducer, @JessicaNorthey, @AmberVines, @ohdoctah, @paul_steele, @AdventureGirl, @JebDickerson, @ImwithJessica, @LoriMoreno, @JulieSpira, @ciaobella50, @AnitaNelson, and @AdamsConsulting.

And finally, a very special thank you to my mother, who said, "Carol, write a book about the *dogs!*"

And so, I did.

About the Author

© RICH MARCHEWKA

Author Carol Quinn is the owner of the social media/PR consultancy ProjectQuinn, and an adjunct faculty member at USC Annenberg School for Communications and Journalism. Carol has written for film and television, and is the co-creator/author of the graphic novel series *Pink Flamingos,* the creator of the YA book series *Palm Beach Prep,* and the author of a new novel, *Under the Ether.* Her second novel is in progress. She has two sons and lives in Southern California.

You can find Carol online at ProjectQuinn.com, 3Lunches.com, www.Facebook.com/FollowMyLeadBook, and FollowMyLeadthe book.com. On Twitter, @ProjectQuinn, @3Lunches, or @FollowMy LeadCQ.

SELECTED TITLES FROM SEAL PRESS

For more than thirty years, Seal Press has published groundbreaking books. By women. For women.

Found: A Memoir, by Jennifer Lauck. $24.95, 978-1-58005-367-9. Picking up where her *NY Times* best-selling memoir, *Blackbird,* left off, Jennifer Lauck shares the powerful story of her search for her birth mother, and lays bare the experience of a woman searching for her identity.

1,000 Mitzvahs: How Small Acts of Kindness Can Heal, Inspire, and Change Your Life, by Linda Cohen. $16.00, 978-1-58005-365-5. When her father passes away, Linda Cohen decides to perform one thousand mitzvahs, or acts of kindness, to honor his memory—and discovers the transformational power of doing good for others.

Second Wind: One Woman's Midlife Quest to Run Seven Marathons on Seven Continents, by Cami Ostman. $16.95, 978-1-58005-307-5. The story of an unlikely athlete and an unlikely heroine: Cami Ostman, a woman edging toward midlife who decides to take on the challenge to run seven marathons on seven continents—and finds herself in the process.

Woman's Best Friend: Women Writers on the Dogs in Their Lives, edited by Megan McMorris. $14.95, 978-1-58005-163-7. An offbeat and poignant collection about those four-legged friends girls can't do without.

Wanderlust: A Love Affair with Five Continents, by Elisabeth Eaves. $16.95, 978-1-58005-311-2. A love letter from the author to the places she's visited—and to the spirit of travel itself—that documents her insatiable hunger for the rush of the unfamiliar and the experience of encountering new people and cultures.

The Quarter-Acre Farm: How I Kept the Patio, Lost the Lawn, and Fed My Family for a Year, by Spring Warren. $16.95, 978-1-58005-340-2. Spring Warren's warm, witty, beautifully-illustrated account of deciding—despite all resistance—to get her hands dirty, create a garden in her suburban yard, and grow 75 percent of all the food her family consumed for one year.

FIND SEAL PRESS ONLINE
www.SealPress.com
www.Facebook.com/SealPress
Twitter: @SealPress